WRITTEN FOR OUR
INSTRUCTION

Written for Our Instruction

Theological and Spiritual Riches in Romans

THOMAS D. STEGMAN, SJ

Paulist Press
New York / Mahwah, NJ

Nihil obstat and Imprimatur
Thomas A. Lawler, SJ
Provincial, Society of Jesus, Wisconsin
September 15, 2016

Cover image : © Lars Justinen—GoodSalt.com
Cover design by Tamian Wood
Book design by Lynn Else

Library of Congress Cataloging-in-Publication Data
Names: Stegman, Thomas, author.
Title: Written for our instruction : theological and spiritual riches in Romans /. Thomas D. Stegman, SJ.
Description: New York : Paulist Press, 2017. | Includes bibliographical references.
Identifiers: LCCN 2016049638 (print) | LCCN 2017015705 (ebook) | ISBN 9781587685286 (Ebook) | ISBN 9780809149377 (pbk. : alk. paper)
Subjects: LCSH: Bible. Romans—Theology. | Catholic Church—Doctrines.
Classification: LCC BS2665.52 (ebook) | LCC BS2665.52 .S745 2017 (print) | DDC 227/.106—dc23
LC record available at https://lccn.loc.gov/2016049638

ISBN 978-0-8091-4937-7 (paperback)
ISBN 978-1-58768-528-6 (e-book)

Published by Paulist Press
997 Macarthur Boulevard
Mahwah, New Jersey 07430
www.paulistpress.com

Printed and bound in the
United States of America

I dedicate this book to my sister, Patricia Hasty.
She has taught me a great deal about the
"work of faith and labor of love and steadfastness
of hope" (1 Thess 1:3). Since being diagnosed with
Multiple Sclerosis in 1994, Patti has been a pillar of
perseverance and strength as a wife, mother, daughter,
and sister. She embodies what Paul wrote in
2 Cor 4:10-11 about carrying in the body the
suffering of Christ (cf. Col 1:24), trusting that she is
participating in the paschal mystery, that mystery
through which God brings life through our various
sufferings and dyings. For her faithful witness to the
power of God's grace, I offer these pages as
a small token of my love and appreciation.

CONTENTS

ACKNOWLEDGMENTS

This book began as a series of articles I wrote for *The Pastoral Review* in 2015 and 2016. At the time, I was writing a pastoral commentary on Paul's Letter to the Romans. In the process of analyzing the letter, I thought it would be beneficial to gather and summarize its main themes in a five-part series. The chapters in this book are significant expansions of those essays. A heartfelt word of thanks goes to Rev. Dr. Michael Hayes, the editor of *The Pastoral Review*, for his permission to use and develop them. I also want to express my gratitude to Paulist Press for encouraging me to write this book.

Thomas D. Stegman, SJ
Feast of the Exaltation of the Holy Cross

INTRODUCTION

Near the end of his Letter to the Romans, Paul sets forth his appreciation for the ongoing power of God's Word as revealed in Scripture: "For whatever was written in former days was written for our instruction, so that by steadfastness and by the encouragement of the scriptures we might have hope" (15:4). The context of Paul's comment is his exhortation to the Christ-believers in Rome to commit themselves to mutual support and edification. They are to expand the horizons of their concern beyond themselves, seeking to do what is best for their neighbors. Paul holds up before the community the example of Jesus Christ as one who "did not please himself" (Rom 15:3), but who came to give his life in love for others (cf. Gal 2:20; Eph 5:2). He then bolsters his reference to Christ by citing a passage from Psalm 69: "The insults of those who insult you have fallen on me" (v. 9).

Why does Paul appeal to Psalm 69, a lament psalm? It recounts the plight of a "servant" of God (69:17) whose zeal for and fidelity to God and his ways are met with derision and insults. The servant appeals to God's steadfast love and mercy for deliverance from his foes. The psalm ends with the servant expressing his confidence that God does in fact hear the cries of the faithful who are in distress.

1

Written for Our Instruction

What is striking is that Paul puts the words of Psalm 69 on the lips of Jesus. That is, he interprets the words of the psalm as pertaining to Jesus. More specifically, he reads Psalm 69 as telling the story of Jesus, whose faithfulness to God and whose love for human beings led to his suffering and death on the cross. But suffering is not the last word. As the servant in the psalm expressed confidence that God would deliver him from harm, so God vindicated Jesus's fidelity and love by raising him from the dead and exalting him in glory. Although Psalm 69 was written centuries before the time of Jesus, its full meaning is revealed in his life, death, and resurrection.

Therefore, Paul can insist that what "was written in former days was written for our instruction." Yet the Scriptures—which, for Paul (as for Jesus), consisted of what Christians regard as the Old Testament—not only find their fulfillment in Christ. They also speak to the situation of the Apostle and the churches to which he wrote. In this instance, Paul wants the Roman faithful to appreciate that they are to participate in Jesus's way of self-giving love, being willing to sacrifice themselves for others. They can do so with confidence, trusting in God to strengthen and vindicate them—especially in the face of misunderstanding and opposition. This is what the Scriptures, here expressed in Psalm 69, bear witness to and teach. They offer encouragement to be steadfast in following the way of Jesus, as well as hope.

Today, Christians read Paul's Letter to the Romans as divinely inspired, as part of the canon of the New Testament. The conviction behind this book is that this letter, though penned nearly two thousand years ago to a specific group of believers, *was also written for our instruction*; hence the title. As Sacred Scripture, Romans—along with the other writings attributed to the Apostle—is a living word that speaks with as much relevance today as when it was first written. It contains much food for thought, for theological and spiritual reflection. The purpose of this book is to give a flavor of these theological and spiritual riches.

Among my motivations for writing, three in particular are worth highlighting. First, from my pastoral experience, I have found that many Catholics are not familiar with Paul's writings. There are understandable reasons for this. One is the way the three-year lectionary cycle—which has been a great blessing, offering "a more ample, more varied, and more suitable reading from Sacred Scripture" (*Sacrosanctum Concilium* 35.1)—is designed for the eucharistic liturgies in Ordinary Time. It presents a semicontinuous reading of the Gospels, with the first reading (from the Old Testament) chosen to correspond, either via parallel or contrast, with the passage from the Gospel proclaimed. However, the second reading, which is usually from the Pauline corpus, has its own cycle of semicontinuous reading. The result is that the content of the second reading does not always fit with the theme(s) of the Gospel and first reading. It can be challenging for homilists to incorporate the second reading into their preaching.

Indeed, the Catholic liturgy privileges the four Gospels. We rise and stand for the Gospel and sing the "Alleluia." Many parishes use a special Book of the Gospels, ornately adorned, for the proclamation by the priest or deacon. It is fair to say that Catholic liturgical practice makes the Gospels the "canon within the canon," the part of the Bible to which we give most prominent attention. And this is not unreasonable, since the Gospels set forth the life and teaching of Jesus, culminating in the events of Holy Week and Easter. But a consequence is the relegation of Paul's writings to lesser attention and focus. My hope is that this book, through its focus on the Letter to the Romans, gives readers a framework for listening to and understanding the reading of *all* Paul's letters at liturgy.

A second motivation for writing is that Paul's letters are not easy—especially in the case of Romans. In the famous, if understated, words of 2 Peter 3:16, "There are some things in [Paul's letters] hard to understand." Since the time of the Reformation, Paul's writings have been the source of much theological controversy. An example is Martin Luther's emphasis on *sola fide*. What precisely does Paul mean by the concept of "justification by faith alone"? What is the relationship for him between faith and works? More recently, scholars have argued over the meaning of his use of the phrases *dikaiosynē theou* ("righteousness of God") and *pistis Christou* ("faith/fulness in" or "of Christ"). In addition, some people struggle with his unrelenting stress on Jesus's cross. This book will give clarity to these and other issues.

A third motivation is the inspired and challenging papacy of Pope Francis. As I write these words, we are observing the Holy Year of Mercy. In the papal bull *Misericordiae Vultus* (The Face of Mercy), which announced the jubilee year, Francis's first biblical reference is Pauline (MV 1; Eph 2:4), where God is described as "rich in mercy." The Pope also cites Romans 11:32, where Paul writes of God's desire to bestow mercy on all people (MV 18). As we will note, God's compassionate mercy is a key theme in Romans, one the Church and world need to hear so desperately. Francis's encyclical *Laudato Si'* (Praise Be to You) is a moving summons to care for the earth God has given to all peoples and creatures for their "home." Paul's portrayal of Christ as the new Adam (Rom 5:15–21) who has ushered in a "new creation" (2 Cor 5:17; Gal 6:15) is most germane for Christians to reflect on how being good stewards of creation should be an essential expression of their discipleship.

Francis's apostolic exhortation on love in the family, *Amoris Laetitia* (The Joy of Love), concludes with his insistence that "mercy is the fullness of justice and the most radiant manifestation of God's truth" (AL 311). This document contains the Pope's beautiful homiletic exposition of Paul's teaching on love in I Corinthians 13:4–7 (AL 90–119; cf. Rom 12:9–21). It also appeals to his teaching about the need for "discerning the body" of Christ (I Cor 11:29; cf. Rom 12:5)—understood as appreciating the social character of the eucharistic celebration, including the need to be sensitive and responsive to the poor and suffering (AL 185–86). In these ways and others, Francis draws on issues and themes from Paul's writings, a good reason for setting forth some basics of the Apostle's theology and spirituality via Romans.

In the pages that follow, our focus will be on what Paul has to say about theology (Who is God?), Christology (Who is Jesus?), pneumatology (What does Paul say about the Holy Spirit?), soteriology (about salvation?), and ecclesiology (about the Church?). Although these five topics are not an exhaustive systematic analysis of the Letter to the Romans, they do capture, in my opinion, his major concerns. Each chapter begins with a passage that illustrates what Paul has to say about the topic in question. I then develop each topic via a four-part explanation. Readers should keep in mind, however, that there is no substitute for reading and studying Romans—as well as the entire Pauline corpus.

Why single out Romans? Given the limited parameters of this book, it will be helpful to concentrate primarily on one letter. And the Letter to the Romans is particularly apt for such a focus. It is the only (undisputed) letter written by Paul to a community he did not found. Though he knew many of the believers who, at the time, were living in the various house churches in Rome (e.g., Prisca and Aquila; cf. Rom 16:3–4; I Cor 16:19), he had not yet visited the capital city of the empire. This letter afforded Paul the opportunity to set forth in a systematic, sustained fashion "the gospel of God" (Rom 1:1) he proclaims, especially for those who had not yet met him. What we thus have in Romans is his most thorough presentation of what God has done through Christ and is doing through the Spirit.

The Letter to the Romans, however, does not contain the entirety of Paul's theology (e.g., there is no reference to the Eucharist in it). I will therefore supplement my exposition at times by drawing from other letters—especially 1–2 Corinthians, Galatians, and Philippians.[1] In addition, I will appeal in places to Ephesians and Colossians, two letters that, because of some stylistic and theological differences, are regarded by many scholars as coming after Paul's death, responding to new situations and circumstances. Even if these letters do in fact postdate Paul (scholars are fairly evenly divided), they are still "Pauline" in the sense of being true to the Apostle's outlook and spirit.[2]

While some issues addressed by Paul can seem to be cemented entirely to the past (for example, disputes over food regulations and the celebration of Jewish feasts; cf. Rom 14:1–6), there is a timeless wisdom in his responses. And as observed above, for those who read his letters as "the Word of God," that is, as divine revelation, this Word is "living and active" (Heb 4:12) today and beyond. Hence it is most appropriate for us to turn to them—and not the least to Romans—to seek their theological and spiritual sustenance. As was the case with Psalm 69 (and for all the Jewish Scriptures of old), they were written for our instruction.

1

GOD

*The gifts and the calling of God are irrevocable....God has
imprisoned all in disobedience so that he may be merciful to all.*

—Romans 11:29, 32

In Romans 9–11, Paul engages in a long and complex defense of
God and the reliability of his Word. The context is a situation
in the early missionary movement that pained the Apostle, cutting
him to the heart. The proclamation of the gospel concerning Jesus,
the crucified-and-risen Jewish Messiah, was not gaining much
acceptance among the Jews, whom Paul calls "my kindred according
to the flesh" (9:3).[1] Rather, the majority of those who were
welcoming the gospel into their hearts were Gentiles. But weren't
the Israelites God's special people? Hadn't God made promises to
them? What did the (for the most part) Jewish rejection of the
gospel, the gospel which Paul had come to see as the fulfillment of
those promises (15:8; cf. 2 Cor 1:20), say about God and his ways?
Had "the word of God" failed vis-à-vis Israel (9:6)?

Paul argues that God's manner of choosing and forming a
people has always possessed a mysterious quality. Israel's refusal (in

Paul's time) led to the gospel being proclaimed to the Gentiles, to peoples who formerly were not even looking to God to be saved. But this does not mean that God has turned his back on the Jews. To the contrary, Paul insists that God's gifts and call to them are irrevocable; the divine promises are eminently trustworthy. Israel's present "disobedience" is, in God's inscrutable ways, serving a life-giving purpose. But in the end, God desires to be merciful to all—to both Gentiles *and* Jews. God remembers his covenant, one that involves the forgiveness of sins (11:27; cf. Jer 31:33–34; Isa 27:9). Mercy marks God's dealings with his people.

The climactic verses of Paul's defense of God's ways capture a number of important elements of his portrayal in Romans of who God is. First, he highlights the "righteousness of God" (1:17), that is, God's covenant faithfulness and saving justice. Second, Paul insists that love and mercy undergird God's righteousness. Third, he presents God as Creator, the giver of life, who raised Jesus from the dead and who offers salvation—the fullness of life—to all people. Fourth, he depicts God as actively involved in history, forming a people and working through them.

DIKAIOSYNĒ THEOU– "RIGHTEOUSNESS OF GOD"

Commentators who carefully analyze the Letter to the Romans are in agreement that 1:16–17 is, in effect, the thesis statement of the entire document. There Paul declares that in the gospel—the message about what God has done in and through Jesus Christ— "the righteousness of God (*dikaiosynē theou*) is revealed." This assertion is the key point he then "unpacks" in the course of writing the letter. Paul returns to this point explicitly in 3:21–22, where he proclaims that "the righteousness of God has been disclosed."

Thus it is evident that the "righteousness of God" is very important for understanding this letter. It is also pivotal for appreciating all of the Apostle's theology.

But what precisely does Paul mean when using this phrase? Here we enter choppy and controversial theological waters. The Greek word *dikaiosynē*, rendered "righteousness," is part of a word group closely associated with the notion of justification. In fact, the related verb *dikaioō* is usually translated "justify." Since the time of the Reformation—when the theological doctrine "justification by faith alone" (*sola fide*) became prominent—most exegetes took *dikaiosynē theou* to mean something concerning human beings as they stood in relation to God as judge. That is, it was thought to refer in the first place to human beings.

This understanding could then have a variety of different nuances. It could refer to a status or a condition bestowed by God on the one who believes in the gospel proclamation. According to some, innocence (righteous standing) was merely imputed by God; according to others, it was actually imparted. The "righteousness of God" was thought by still other exegetes to refer to a quality a person has that is then recognized by God. In some construals, the quality was something that actually belonged to the person; in other construals, it was first given to the believer by God and then recognized by him. In all these instances, the phrase "righteousness of God" is understood as pertaining to a human being—observe the emphasis on the individual—before God.

But is this what *Paul* means? It is striking that, at the beginning of the letter and again near its end, he employs the phrase "the gospel of God" (1:1; 15:16). The Letter to the Romans is about the saving activity of God, whose outreach encompasses all peoples and the whole of creation. It concerns what God has done, is doing, and will do through Christ and the gift of the Spirit. Over one third of Paul's explicit references to God (*theos*) in the undisputed letters are found in Romans. It is no exaggeration to claim that the major protagonist in this letter is God. More recently, a growing number of scholars have pushed back against the anthropological interpretation of *dikaiosynē theou*, and insisted on a more properly *theological* understanding. In other words, they contend (rightly, in my opinion) that the phrase refers to *God*, to God's own righteousness. It signifies both an attribute of God and the activity that emanates from this attribute.

This attribute can be expressed as faithfulness or fidelity. Elsewhere Paul uses the word *pistos* ("faithful") to describe God (1 Cor 1:9; 10:13; 2 Cor 1:18). Most fundamentally, God's righteousness connotes God's faithfulness—his faithfulness to creation and, even more, to his covenant promises. As we will see, God seeks to form a people who bear witness to his holiness and ways. God's righteousness is thus closely linked to his role as Creator and covenant God. For this reason, many commentators refer to God's *covenant faithfulness*. Hence, there *is* a relational aspect to God's righteousness. But notice that the Apostle's emphasis is on God's integrity and commitment to his creation and—most especially—to people with whom he desires to be in a special relationship.

While the notion of covenant faithfulness conveys much of what Paul means by the phrase *dikaiosynē theou*, it does not exhaust its meaning. God's righteousness also refers to divine justice. This meaning became enshrined following the influential translation of St. Jerome, who translated the Greek New Testament into Latin (part of the text known as the Vulgate[2]). Jerome rendered the phrase in question as *iustitia Dei*. In describing God's role as judge, Paul declares that "God shows no partiality" (2:11). God "will repay according to each one's deeds" (2:6)—eternal life to those who do good and seek God's glory; anguish and distress to those who choose wickedness and are self-seeking. God's justice is thus marked by complete and utter fairness. Related to this is Paul's insistence on the oneness of God (3:30). Since God is one, the same God of both Jews and Gentiles, he has reached out to "justify" (*dikaioō*)—to bring into right relationship—all peoples by the same means, namely through his Son Jesus Christ.

The latter observation anticipates the answer to this question: What does God, who is characterized by covenant faithfulness and justice, do in the face of human rebellion and sin? While Paul recognizes the special role of the Israelites in God's plan—as well as their privileged status as covenant partners (cf. 9:4–5)—he nevertheless insists that *all* peoples have the ability to know God as Creator and to respond to him with thanksgiving and honor (1:19–21). However, "all have sinned and fall short of the glory of God" (3:23). And in rebelling against God, human beings—by participating in Adam's primordial disobedience—became ensnared by the powers of sin and death (5:12), which Paul conceives as malevolent cosmic powers that mercilessly enslave and kill. Having rebelled and sinned, human beings were rendered helpless, unable to extricate themselves from the consequences of their rejection of God.

The remarkable aspect of God's righteousness is herein revealed. Undoubtedly, human rebellion and sin are an affront to God's holiness. But Paul teaches that God's sense of justice, though perfectly impartial and fair, contains another crucially important aspect. God's justice is also a *saving* justice, which is another way of understanding what Paul means by *dikaiosynē theou*. In response to the condition of universal sinfulness, Paul teaches that God did not stand back and do nothing. Rather, God acted through his Son, Jesus Christ, to condemn the insidious, enslaving power of sin (8:3) and to offer to human beings the gifts of redemption and forgiveness (3:24–25). God's righteousness is such that, through Christ, he creates the possibility of restoring proper relationships through reconciliation. God makes right what had gone wrong because of human infidelity and injustice (3:3–7). God is ever faithful to being in covenant relationship.

God's righteousness has been revealed most dramatically through Jesus's death on the cross (3:21–26), a death that for Paul was the climactic manifestation of the Son's self-giving love (cf. Gal 2:20). In restoring to right relationship those who receive his offer of salvation through Christ, God not only forgives their transgressions and declares them innocent, he also makes them righteous (3:26; 5:19). We will return to these points in chapter 4, but for now let us dwell a moment on the notion of God's making people righteous. This refers to God's empowerment to participate in the dynamism of self-giving love that led Jesus to offer his life on the cross. One of Paul's most remarkable statements is found in 2 Corinthians 5:21, where he declares that God has acted through Christ "so that in him we might become the righteousness of God." In other words, God's character is to be reflected in the lives of those whom he has saved. Paul can therefore exhort, "Be imitators of God…and live in love, as Christ loved us and gave himself up for us" (Eph 5:1–2). God's righteousness thereby *continues* to be revealed.

LOVE AND MERCY: GOD'S ESSENTIAL ATTRIBUTES

While God's righteousness is undoubtedly a central theme in Romans, it is not the only divine attribute Paul highlights. The previous section has already offered hints of two of them—love and mercy. Love is the attribute that undergirds God's righteousness. Mercy is the ultimate expression of God's love. Together, as Pope Francis continually reminds us, love and mercy bring us to the heart of the very mystery of who God is.

Explicit references to God's love (*agapē*) in Romans are, admittedly, not numerous (5:5, 8; 8:39). But here is a case where quantitative lexical analysis—looking at the number of times a certain word is used—can be misleading. Paul's references to divine love form a bracket around a major section of the letter (5:1—8:39) that spells out the ramifications of God's intervention to make right what had gone wrong because of human sin. The Apostle's central point is that God shows his love in that he "did not withhold his own Son, but gave him up for all of us" (8:32). God's love has no limits. God holds nothing back, not even his beloved Son, in reaching out to save. And notice that God's desire is that *all* people be saved (cf. 1 Tim 2:4); the scope of God's love is universal. Nearly a half century later, Paul's teaching would be echoed by the author of the Fourth Gospel: "For God so loved the world that he gave his only Son, so that everyone who believes in him may not perish but may have eternal life" (John 3:16).

The greatness and magnanimity of God's love are evident in that he revealed it most dramatically—through Jesus's offering himself on the cross—"while we still were sinners" (5:8), in the condition of being "ungodly" (5:6). Divine love is thus pure *charis*, a term that means "gift" and "grace." God's love is not something we have to earn or merit. Rather, it is the basis that makes possible our response of love—for God and for others. The reconciling, life-giving love of God is also formidable, "much more" powerful than the forces of sin and death (see the comparisons in 5:15–19). Through his love, God shows that he is fundamentally on our side: God is *for* us. As Paul triumphantly exclaims, "If God is for us, who is against us?" (8:31). Indeed, there is nothing that "will be able to separate us from the love of God in Christ Jesus" (8:39). God's love is thus revealed to be the most powerful force there is, stronger than death itself. No wonder that Paul refers to the gospel as God's "power" (*dynamis*; the word from which we get "dynamite") for salvation (1:16).

Moreover, God's love *continues* to be expressed through the outpouring of the Holy Spirit in the hearts of those who receive the gospel proclamation (5:5). Paul describes this gift of divine love as "dwelling" or, better, "taking up residence" (the verb is *oikeō*, from

13

the word for "house," *oikos*) in the human heart (8:9–11). This is a mystery worthy of much contemplation and awe. The Spirit who mediates God's love enables people to call out to him as "Abba" (8:15), the same term of intimacy Jesus used when he prayed to God as Father (Mark 14:36; cf. Gal 4:6). Those who were formerly God's enemies because of sin (5:10) now have the status of "beloved" (1:7) and God's children (8:16). Such is the transforming power of God's love, mediated through Christ and the Spirit. Paul is the one who has given us the liturgical blessing: "The grace of the Lord Jesus Christ, the love of God, and the communion of the Holy Spirit be with all of you" (2 Cor 13:13). The "hinge" in this blessing is God's love.

While God's love functions to frame the content of chapters 5—8, the theme of divine mercy becomes prominent beginning in chapter 9 (cf. 9:15–16, 18, 23; 11:30–32; 12:1; 15:9). Paul employs two related terms—*eleos* ("mercy") and *oiktirmos* ("compassion")—to express it.

He refers to God's mercy in making his *apologia* for God's faithfulness to Israel in the section referred to at the beginning of this chapter. Recounting the history of God's dealings with Israel, Paul cites the divine revelation to Moses following the incident of the golden calf (cf. Exod 32): "I will have mercy on whom I have mercy, / and I will have compassion on whom I have compassion" (9:15; cf. Exod 33:19). This revelation foreshadows the creedal-like divine self-manifestation found in Exodus 34:6: "The LORD, the LORD, / a God merciful and gracious, / slow to anger, / and abounding in steadfast love and faithfulness." Paul, the former Pharisee who was steeped in the Jewish Scriptures, holds fast to this foundational characterization of God as merciful and compassionate.

Paul alludes to the divine mercy toward Israel as revealed in the fact that, even in the worst of the people's infidelities, God has continually left behind a remnant of Israelites who were faithful to him (cf. 9:27–29). The point is that God does not abandon his people. Paul also highlights the mercy God is presently showing to Gentiles by having the gospel proclaimed to them. In fact, Paul's own vocation is to "proclaim [Christ] among the Gentiles" (Gal 1:16). Vis-à-vis his fellow Jews, he remains confident that God will bestow his mercy on "all Israel" (11:26, 31). It is no accident that, when setting forth the manner of life that is the appropriate response to the gospel, Paul begins his exhortations by invoking "the mercies of God" (12:1). By continually referring to divine mercy, he reinforces that God's righteousness is grounded in love, and God's justice is rooted in mercy.

Now, it might be objected that the foregoing treatment is narrowly one-sided. Doesn't Paul also emphasize "the wrath (*orgē*) of God" in Romans? To be sure, in the verse immediately following the initial reference to God's righteousness, he declares that God's wrath is also being revealed (1:18). But it is crucial to appreciate that divine wrath is not some vindictive or arbitrary force. Instead, Paul suggests that the wrath of God alludes to his permitting people to suffer the destructive consequences of rejecting him and his ways. Rather than indicate tyranny or pettiness on God's part, divine "wrath" and "severity" (*apotomia*; 11:22) refer to the allowed outcomes for those who, rather than obey the Creator God, insist on grasping after "life" on their own terms—an insistence that ultimately leads to death.

Following his description of the revelation of God's wrath (1:18–32), Paul makes clear that God is ultimately characterized by his "kindness and forbearance and patience" (2:4). This portrayal challenges false, unhealthy images of God—for instance, that of a harsh, unmerciful scorekeeper of faults and failings. The term translated "kindness" is *chrēstotēs*, which denotes uprightness and trustworthiness in one's relationships, in addition to helpfulness and generosity. God's forbearance (*anochē*) and patience (*makrothymia*) are closely related to the divine impetus toward clemency, to offering second chances and to making right what has gone wrong. But it is crucial to appreciate that these divine qualities are directed toward *repentance*. God's patience and forbearance should never be regarded as his indifference toward human injustice, greed, exploitation, and the like. Rather, they invite a change of mind and heart (the meaning of *metanoia*) toward God and his ways.

Paul fills out his portrait of God with a few more descriptions. He depicts God as the "God of steadfastness and encouragement" (15:5). God's steadfastness (*hypomonē*) is another way of expressing his ongoing faithfulness to creation and to his covenant promises. The word rendered "encouragement," *paraklēsis*, is derived from *parakaleō*, a verb rich in connotation. It means, literally, "call alongside," and can be translated "comfort" or "console." The "God of encouragement" conveys an image of God who invites people to draw close to him to receive his help and consolation. It should therefore come as no surprise that Paul refers to God as the "God of peace" (15:33; 16:20) and the "God of hope" (15:13)— that is, as the one who is able to bestow true contentment and to fulfill our deepest longings and aspirations.

GOD THE CREATOR AND SUSTAINER WHO GIVES LIFE TO THE DEAD

Paul draws on the tradition of God as Creator, the maker of all things and giver of life. He alludes to this tradition in his description of God as the one—and the *only* one—who "calls into existence the things that do not exist" (4:17). Observe that Paul employs the present tense verb "calls." God's creative power is not limited to what he did "in the beginning" when he created the world (cf. Gen 1:1); it *continues* to be at work, sustaining in each and every moment, in each and every second, all that exists. St. Ignatius of

Loyola captures God's creative, sustaining power in his "Contemplation on Divine Love" at the end of the *Spiritual Exercises*. There he describes God as laboring to give being to and conserve everything in the heavens and on the earth, and how we are the beneficiaries of this loving, creative power. This fundamental truth humbles—we are not God. It also exalts—God has done great things for us. The fact that God is constantly at work is also a reminder of the need to be alert to God's presence and activity in our lives.

Near the beginning of the letter, Paul refers to God's work of creation in arguing that *all* peoples should be able to discern and give glory to God the Creator: "Ever since the creation of the world his eternal power and divine nature, invisible though they are, have been understood and seen through the things he has made" (1:20). The Apostle's point is made more eloquently by the Jesuit poet Gerard Manley Hopkins in the opening line of "God's Grandeur": "The world is charged with the grandeur of God." The beauty of nature—mountains, trees, rivers, flowers, and birds, not to mention the skies—is revelatory of God's artistic, creative power. Much spiritual fruit can be gained by having one's eyes, ears, and nose attuned to the created order, and then giving honor and thanks to God its maker (cf. 1:21). This way of encountering God's presence and power is often underappreciated, however, whether because of our inattentiveness, our lack of care for creation, or our preference for mediating reality through handheld devices.

Elsewhere, Paul insists on the *goodness* of the created order. In discussing the propriety of eating meat sold in the market place— meat that *may* have been involved in pagan sacrificial rites—he cites the opening line of Psalm 24: "Eat whatever is sold in the meat market without raising any question on the ground of conscience, for 'the earth and its fullness are the Lord's'" (1 Cor 10:25–26). All that God has made is good and should thus be received with thanksgiving. Moreover, Paul presumes the biblical teaching that human beings are created in God's image and have been given the privilege to participate in bringing new life into the world and in caring for creation (Gen 1:26–28). In response to God the giver of life, we are to be thoroughly committed to life, to be "pro-life" in the full sense of the term. This includes not only protecting human life from conception to natural death, but also—as Pope Francis insists in his encyclical, *Laudato Si'*—taking radical measures of conversion in order to restore, safeguard, and pass on to future generations the blessings of our "common home."

Returning to Romans, Paul sets forth the tragedy of human rebellion against God the Creator in 1:18–23. The problem is idolatry, the failure to worship God and the giving allegiance to that which is not God: "They exchanged the glory of the immortal God for images resembling a mortal human being or birds or four-footed animals or reptiles" (1:23). Today, it is easy to think that idols are a relic of the past. Be that as it may, idolatry is rampant. It occurs whenever I put someone (often myself) or something ahead of God. A good self-examination in this connection is to ask myself on what/whom do I expend my time, my energy, and my resources—and why do I do so? The answers may reveal what/who are my gods. According to Paul, the consequences of "all ungodliness and wickedness" (1:18) are dire, especially the complete and bitter rupture of human relationships (1:29–31). Today we can add the exploitation of the environment with its subsequent subjection to "futility" and to "bondage to decay" (8:20–21).

God's life-giving power, however, is not thwarted. Paul declares that the one who "calls into existence the things that do not exist" is also the one "who gives life to the dead" (4:17; cf. 2 Cor 1:9). Recall what was said above about the formidable power of God's love. Through the cross of his Son Jesus, God has defeated the death-dealing power of sin. The victory of life is revealed, in the first place, by the resurrection of Jesus. A striking feature of Romans is the number of times Paul refers to God's raising Jesus from the dead to eschatological life—that is, to the fullness of life

(4:24–25; 6:4; 8:11; 10:9). That God raised Jesus echoes like a mantra as one reads the letter, reminding us throughout that God desires to bestow the fullness of life on all who turn to him to be saved.

Through the life, death, and resurrection of Jesus, God has inaugurated the new creation (2 Cor 5:17; Gal 6:15). Paul alludes to Adam's disobedience (Gen 3) when declaring that "as all die in Adam, so all will be made alive in Christ" (1 Cor 15:22). The one who makes alive, of course, is God. Christ is "the first fruits" of the resurrection (1 Cor 15:23), presaging the future glorification of God's adopted children (8:29–30). But it is not just human beings who will be transformed into the fullness of the new creation. *All* creation will be liberated and renewed (8:21). God's life-giving power will prevail, as does his faithfulness to what he has created. Just as our belief in the resurrection of the body gives theological grounding and motivation for respecting the dignity of embodied human existence, so should the Apostle's teaching about the renewal of creation give such grounding and motivation for caring for the environment and all that is contained therein.

While Paul speaks of the fullness of resurrection life as a future reality, he also makes it clear that God's salvific, life-giving power has present ramifications (cf. 6:4–5). Salvation will be the subject of a subsequent chapter. For now, it will be sufficient to mention in brief the various metaphors Paul employs to convey God's gift of new life through the death and resurrection of Jesus. In 3:24–25, he refers to "the redemption that is in Christ Jesus, whom God put forward as a sacrifice of atonement." "Redemption" evokes the cultural reality (in Paul's time) of the buying back or ransoming of a family member who had been captured and enslaved. Here it refers to God's gift of true freedom from the malevolent forces of sin and death. "Sacrifice of atonement" points to the forgiveness of sins, the effect of which was compared to two related images: relief from a heavy physical burden (e.g., Ps 38:4) and release from a debt (e.g., Matt 18:23–35).

In 5:9–10, Paul declares, "Much more surely then, now that we have been justified by [Christ's] blood....For if while we were enemies, we were reconciled to God through the death of his Son." Reconciliation, as we have seen, signifies the healing of a broken relationship with God. Justification, in addition to connoting a declaration of "innocence," also entails God's conferral of the status of membership in his covenant people. The latter is in fulfillment of God's promises to Abraham of a family whose distinguishing mark is faithfulness (cf. 4:13–16). In all these ways, the saving God creates the possibility for people to be alive to him (6:11). And being alive to God—the one who creates and brings the dead to life—is to be truly alive.

GOD'S INVOLVEMENT WITH PEOPLE AND IN HISTORY

God's role as Creator means more than making the heavens and the earth and all that is contained therein. God also creates a *people*, shaping and forming them for a special purpose. In the first place, Paul insists on the special role played by his fellow people, the Jews. He suggests Israel's unique role in salvation history by the phrase "the Jew first and also the Greek" ("Greek" is used here as synecdoche for "Gentile" or non-Jew; cf. 1:16; 2:9, 10). This role is also evoked by the extended reference to Abraham in 4:1–25.

Paul's use of the Abraham story is complex and multifaceted. He draws on the narrative in Genesis in which God's call to Abraham (Gen 12:1–3) follows the story of the tower of Babel (Gen 11:1–9). Babel is a story of human rebellion against God (expressed by the attempt to build a tower to scale the heavens) that resulted in the fracturing of the human race (signified by the scattering of peoples and the confusion caused by different languages). God's call to

Abraham illustrates the divine impetus to get involved in history in order to make right what has gone wrong. God's promises to Abraham of numerous descendants and a land (cf. 4:13)—realized first in the people God gathered at Sinai following the exodus from Egypt—reveals the divine plan to work in and through a people. As we have seen, God is covenantal.

Paul had to reassess many of the convictions he previously held as a Pharisee (cf. Phil 3:5) in light of his encounter with the risen Christ. Nevertheless, he maintains that Israel was called as a people to be "a guide to the blind, a light to those who are in darkness, a corrector of the foolish, a teacher of children, having in the law the embodiment of knowledge and truth" (2:19–20). The Mosaic Law, given at Sinai, is a great blessing for Jews, teaching them how to live as God's holy people. Indeed, fundamental to Israel's vocation is to show forth God's holiness and ways to the nations, as the just-quoted text shows (cf. Lev 19:2: "You shall be holy, for I the LORD your God am holy"). Instead of being a burden and constraint, the Law is an empowering gift and revelation from God. It is crucial for Christians to have an appreciation for what the Law meant, and means today, for Jews.

The Law is one of many gifts bestowed on Israel. They "were entrusted with the oracles of God" (3:2), a reference to the Scriptures. Another gift is their adoption as God's children (9:4; cf. Hos 11:1). God relates to his people as a loving Father. They have also been given "the glory, the covenants,...the worship, and the promises; to them belong the patriarchs" (9:4–5). God's commitment to his people, moreover, was not exhausted by the giving of gifts. Even when Israel disobeyed the ways of God and suffered various calamities, including exile, he remained in relationship, preserving a faithful remnant.

After his encounter with the risen Jesus, Paul reassessed what, or better *who*, was the greatest of God's gifts to Israel: namely, "the Messiah" (9:5). The coming of Jesus—whom the Apostle came to appreciate was not only the Jewish Messiah but also God's Son, the personal manifestation and expression of God—is the climax of divine involvement in history to make right what had gone wrong through human rebellion. Paul regards Christ[3] Jesus as "the end of the law" (10:4), a phrase that must be carefully understood. While the term *telos* can mean "end" as termination point, it can also connote the notion of "goal" and "fulfillment." And while Paul at times employs *nomos* to signify the "law" (that is, the commandments), he also uses it to refer to the entire story set forth in Scripture (including in the first five books, attributed to Moses, known as the "Torah").

Putting these points together, Paul regards Jesus as the *telos*, the goal and fulfillment of the Jewish Scriptures. Christ is the one through whom all God's promises have been fulfilled. In fact, it is no accident that Paul lists the "patriarchs" and "promises" immediately preceding the Messiah (9:4–5). Jesus is the climax of the story told in the Jewish Scriptures. Moreover, Jesus fulfills the Law/Torah in the sense that his faithfulness to God and his self-giving love for people embody the holiness that the Jewish Law/Torah intends. Jesus is the faithful Israelite through whom God has acted to bring about reconciliation and peace.

But that is not the end of the story. No, God *continues* to draw near and be involved with people and in history. Returning to the figure of Abraham, Paul reads the promise to him that "in you all the families of the earth shall be blessed" (Gen 12:3) as referring to the inclusion of the Gentiles into God's people (Gal 3:8). He came to see that the descendants promised to Abraham include *both* Jews and Gentiles, whose distinguishing characteristic is faithfulness (4:11–12, 16). Now, through the gospel proclamation, "power of God for salvation" can be experienced by all—Jews (like Paul) and Gentiles—who receive the good news with faith (1:16). Those who respond with faith are the *ekklēsia*, literally the ones "called forth" by God. They are the "family" of God the Father who are enabled to take on, more and more, the likeness of Jesus, the "firstborn" Son among many brothers and sisters (8:29).

Communities of believers, the Body of Christ (12:5), are now empowered and charged by God's Spirit to show forth to the world his saving power to reconcile people. They are, in effect, the sacrament of God's love (cf. *Lumen Gentium* 48). They are enabled to be the good stewards of creation God intended them to be. Through their mutual service in love (15:2) and their coming together to praise and glorify God (15:7–13), they bear witness to the holiness of God and the power of his kingdom, a reign of "righteousness and peace and joy in the Holy Spirit" (14:17). God's reign of righteousness thereby becomes more and more a reality in space and time, here and now.

"Righteousness"…there's that word again. God's faithfulness is manifested in the coming of Jesus, the sending of the Spirit, and the formation of communities of the faithful that together make up the Church. But what about Israel, the original recipient of the "oracles of God" (3:2)? While Paul was pained by the unbelief of most of his fellow Jews—whom, recall, he regarded and loved as his kin (9:3)—he was also convinced that God's righteousness, his covenant fidelity, remains unshaken: "The gifts and the calling of God are irrevocable" (11:29). The Apostle does not pretend to know all the workings of God. But he trusts in the outworking of God's love, that it will result in God's having mercy upon all (11:32), and that "all Israel will be saved" (11:26).[4] God's Word has not failed. No wonder Paul concludes with a song of praise: "O the depth of the riches and wisdom and knowledge of God!…how inscrutable his ways! /….To him be the glory forever. Amen" (11:33–36).

Paul's doxology is a most fitting way to conclude this study of who God is—the *theology*—in Romans. As a matter of fact, he glorifies, blesses, and thanks God throughout the letter (e.g., 1:25; 7:25; 8:31–39; 9:5; 16:25–27). Such praise is the appropriate response to the God of unfailing faithfulness, infinite love, and abundant mercy. Such honor is due to the Creator and Sustainer of all life. And such blessing is owed to the one who acts through people in history for salvation—in short, to God who is "Abba," the Father of Messiah Jesus. It is to Paul's treatment of Jesus that we turn in the following chapter.

QUESTIONS FOR PRAYER AND REFLECTION

1. How does the interpretation of God's righteousness as "covenant faithfulness" enrich my understanding of who God is? How have I experienced God's faithfulness in my life?

2. When I think of justice vis-à-vis God, what immediately comes to mind? How does the notion of saving justice impact the way I understand the "justice of God"?

3. How do Paul's ways of setting forth the love of God help me to appreciate the extent of God's love for me? For all people?

4. What inspires me most in Paul's teaching about God's mercy and compassion? What does it call forth from me in response?

5. Which of the other divine attributes do I find most consoling? Challenging? Why? Does Paul's exposition call into question my image of God?

6. How does Paul's understanding of God's creation of and sustaining all that exists—including myself—help me to reflect on God's presence in the world? How have I reflected on the divine power and presence manifested in the beauty of creation?

7. In what ways am I called to be a better steward of the gifts of creation? What are the "idols" that can keep me from responding to God's love and care?

8. How have I experienced God's power to bring the dead to life?

9. In what ways does Paul's focus on a people (that is, Israel; the Church)—over and above individuals—illuminate my ways of thinking about how God acts?

10. How does Paul's teaching about God's presence and activity in and through the Church inspire me to think differently about my involvement in a faith community? How might my faith community reach out and relate to a community from another religious tradition (Jewish or otherwise)?

2

JESUS

The gospel concerning [God's] Son, who was descended
from David according to the flesh and was declared to be
Son of God with power according to the spirit of holiness by
resurrection from the dead, Jesus Christ our Lord.

—Romans 1:3–4

All of Paul's letters—both the undisputed ones and those that many scholars regard as written in the Apostle's name after his death—begin with a greeting formula that contains three elements: X (sender), to Y (addressee), "grace and peace" (that is, the greeting itself). Scholars point out that it is illuminating to see how Paul expands on any of these elements. Such expansions foreshadow key themes and topics he then takes up in the course of writing the letter in question. What is striking about the greeting in the Letter to the Romans is its length—seven verses. And six of these are dedicated to describing the sender, Paul! This is due to the fact that he is introducing himself to believers in a city he has yet to visit. Many of the recipients in Rome have not met him.

Paul introduces himself as an apostle who has been "set apart for the gospel of God" (1:1). That is, he has a special vocation to proclaim the gospel. As we saw in the previous chapter, the "gospel of God" is the good news that God has acted in history to bring salvation. Immediately following this initial reference to God's gospel, Paul states that it was "promised beforehand through his prophets in the holy scriptures" (1:2). He then sets forth the fundamental *content* of this gospel, namely Jesus. In the text cited above, Paul offers the earliest scriptural witness to Jesus's Davidic descent, an allusion to his identity as the Messiah (cf. Luke 1:32; 2 Tim 2:8). He also makes clear Jesus's divine Sonship. Moreover, he bears witness to Jesus as Lord, now made manifest in his resurrection from the dead.

This creedal-like statement—some commentators think that Paul is reciting an early formulaic tradition concerning Jesus in 1:3–4—contains many seeds of the Apostle's Christology. First, Paul focuses on Jesus as the Messiah and the Son of God, the personal manifestation of God. Second, Jesus is "Lord" (*kyrios*), the same term used in the Greek translation of the Jewish Scriptures for the divine name. Third, Paul presents Jesus as the fulfillment of Scripture. And fourth, he offers a portrait of Jesus as the new Adam who embodies and empowers authentic human existence.

JESUS THE MESSIAH AND SON OF GOD

The heart of Paul's proclamation of the gospel is that God's righteousness (that is, his covenant fidelity and saving justice) has been definitively revealed *dia pisteōs Iēsou Christou* (3:21–22). As was the case with the meaning of *dikaiosynē theou*, we enter into exegetical and theological controversy over the translation of *pistis Christou*.

Typically, this phrase has been rendered "faith in Christ." Indeed, the NRSV translates 3:22 as follows: "The righteousness of God [has been disclosed] through faith in Jesus Christ for all who believe." However, in a footnote, the NRSV also provides an alternative translation: "through the faith of Jesus Christ." Along with a growing number of interpreters, I prefer a slight emendation of this alternative, translating *pistis* as "faithfulness."

There are a number of compelling reasons for interpreting 3:21–22 as "God's righteousness has been manifested primarily *through the faithfulness of Jesus Christ*" rather than *"through our faith in Christ."* First of all, the entire paragraph (3:21–26) highlights *God's* saving activity; the focus is on what God has done and is doing. Moreover, given the fact that, in the preceding sections, Paul relentlessly establishes the sinfulness and unrighteousness of all humanity (1:18—3:20; cf. 3:23), it is unlikely that he would then immediately turn around and state that human beings' faith is the place where God's righteousness is revealed. The tense of the verb rendered "has been disclosed" is another clue. Paul employs the perfect tense, which in Greek signifies an action in the past that has ongoing ramifications in the present. Finally, the NRSV's translation is peculiarly redundant ("faith...for all who believe").

But what does it mean for Paul to say that God's righteousness has been manifested through the faithfulness of Jesus Christ? Both terms associated here with Jesus—"Christ" and "faithfulness"—are important for Paul. *Christos* is not a surname, as if it were Jesus's family name. Rather, it indicates his identity as the Jewish Messiah (cf. 1:3; "who was descended from David according to the flesh"). The term *Christos* means "the anointed one," the one through whom God has intervened for the sake of salvation (cf. Luke 4:16–21). Paul returns, near the conclusion of the letter, to Jesus's messianic identity and role: "For I tell you that Christ has become a servant of the circumcised [i.e., Israel] on behalf of the truth of God in order that he might confirm the promises given to the patriarchs"

(15:8). Jesus is the Messiah who "came not to be served but to serve, and to give his life a ransom for many" (Mark 10:45). And in doing so, he fulfilled God's covenant faithfulness (cf. the promises) and showed forth God's truthfulness.

Jesus, the promised Messiah, can manifest God's truthfulness because he is God's own Son (8:32). As God's Son, he can do what only God can do. Messiah Jesus was sent by God to break the enslaving power of sin (8:3), which Paul understands to be an oppressive cosmic force (5:12). Jesus does so by his faithfulness to God's will that culminated with his death on the cross. Paul alludes to this fidelity-unto-death in 3:25, a verse notoriously difficult to translate. Literally, it states that Jesus the Messiah is the one "whom God put forward as an expiation, through faith(fulness), by means of his blood." The expression "through faithfulness, by means of his blood" points to Jesus's faithfulness to the Father in offering his life. Through Jesus's death (and resurrection)—events in the past—God has brought about the present possibility of forgiveness of transgressions (4:25) and liberation (3:24) from the enslaving power of sin (recall the force of the perfect tense verb "has been disclosed" in 3:21–22).

Paul alludes to Jesus's faithfulness later in the letter, where he contrasts it with Adam's disobedience: "For just as by the one man's [Adam's] disobedience the many were made sinners, so by the one man's [Christ's] obedience the many will be made righteous" (5:19). Notice how the Apostle focuses exclusively on the Messiah's obedience (hypakoē) in this passage. There is no mention of the human response of faith. This reinforces the interpretation of 3:21–22 that God acts, first and foremost, through Jesus's faithfulness and obedience to his will. Paul's emphasis is both theological and christological. Elsewhere, he refers to Jesus's obedience "to the point of death" in the Christ hymn in Philippians 2:6–11, a passage that is very prominent in the Church's liturgy (it is proclaimed at the Mass on Palm Sunday and prayed every Saturday in the Evening Prayer of the Divine Office). There, Jesus's obedience is part and parcel of his taking on the form of a slave/servant, humbling himself for the sake of others.

It is crucial to appreciate that Jesus's faithfulness/obedience-unto-death is an expression of his *love*. Paul's exposition is at times highly compact. He leaves it to his readers to make explicit what is left implicit. Such is the case in 5:6–8, where he begins by proclaiming, "At the right time Christ died for the ungodly." Then he declares, "God proves his love for us in that while we still were sinners Christ died for us." The implicit logic here is that the Messiah's death for sinners is an expression of God's love *because Jesus offers himself in love* for all people (cf. Gal 2:20; Eph 5:2). This is the love to which Paul refers when asking, "Who will separate us from the love of Christ?" (8:35). The answer is "no one," not even (personified) death. Jesus's filial love for and faithfulness to his Father are manifested most dramatically in his love for all human beings, a love that knows no bounds.

While Paul's exposition places the accent on Jesus's faithfulness and obedience to God, nevertheless he also insists on the necessity of a proper response to the gospel. Recall that the righteousness of God has been revealed through the Messiah's faithfulness "for all who believe" (3:22) or "for all who are faithful" (au. trans.). In the greeting of the letter, Paul explains that his call to be an apostle has as its purpose "to bring about the obedience of faith (*hypakoē pisteōs*)" (1:5). The latter phrase can be variously understood. In my opinion, it is best rendered as the obedience that *is* faith. To be sure, the life of faith begins with believing the good news that God has acted in and through Jesus for our salvation. But *pistis* signifies more than intellectual assent. It also entails putting on Christ by embodying his way of life. At the heart of faith is an intensive, prayerful listening to God's Word. In fact, the verb *akouō*, "listen," is embedded in the word for "obey" (*hypakouō*). Such listening is the seedbed for the Spirit to transform people to take on the likeness of Jesus's faithfulness and obedience.

Paul also refers to Jesus as Messiah in the context of listing the privileges God has bestowed on Israel (9:4–5). This list comes to a climax with reference to the Messiah: "To them belong the patriarchs, and from them, according to the flesh, comes the Messiah." The meaning of what follows—"who is over all, God blessed forever"—is debated by exegetes, as the Greek text can be understood in two different ways. One is that "God" (*theos*) is the predicate of the "Messiah." In this reading (as in the NRSV's translation), Paul equates Jesus the Messiah with God. This interpretation is supported by the fact that he appreciates that Jesus—the Messiah and Son of God—is the personal manifestation of God's saving love. However, because such a direct predication does not appear elsewhere in the Apostle's undisputed letters, some commentators place a full stop after "Messiah," and translate the end of 9:5 as a benediction to God the Father (that is, "God, who is over all, be blessed forever").

JESUS THE LORD

Regardless of how one interprets 9:5, there is no doubt that Paul has a "high" Christology, an assessment of Jesus as divine. This is evident from his use of *kyrios* ("Lord") in connection with Jesus. The word *kyrios* was employed by the translators of the Hebrew Bible into Greek[1] to render the sacred divine name YHWH. To call Jesus *kyrios* is to make a powerful theological statement. Moreover, as we will see below, when quoting Scripture, Paul reads some texts whose original referent was God to refer to Jesus. Interestingly, he often combines the titles of Lord and Messiah when naming Jesus (e.g., 1:7—"the Lord Jesus Christ"; and 5:21—"Jesus Christ our Lord"). This combination is also found in the Introductory Rites of the Mass, where Catholics call on him as "Lord" and "Messiah" when begging for mercy: *Kyrie eleison...Christe eleison...Kyrie eleison.*

Jesus's title as *kyrios* is typically associated with his resurrection. In I Corinthians 9:1, Paul asks, "Am I not an apostle? Have I not seen Jesus our Lord?" This is one of the rare occasions where he speaks of his encounter with the risen Jesus, an encounter that was also his call to proclaim the gospel to the Gentiles (Gal 1:15–16). Prior to that, Paul the Pharisee regarded Jesus as a messianic pretender (cf. 2 Cor 5:16), one whose death by crucifixion had been cursed by God (Gal 3:13; cf. Deut 21:23). But Paul's encounter with Jesus—not only as one brought back to life, but even more as one raised to the fullness of eschatological life and imbued with the very glory of God—led him to reassess who Jesus is and what his crucifixion means. Jesus is Lord, and his death on the cross is for our salvation, expressing the paradoxical power of God's self-giving love. The ongoing power of the risen Lord is evident in the fruit it bore in the Apostle's tireless missionary activity from the moment he was stopped in his tracks on the road to Damascus.

As we saw at the outset of this chapter, Paul makes the association of Jesus's Lordship with the resurrection in the greetings of Romans: "[Who] was declared to be Son of God with power according to the spirit of holiness by resurrection from the dead, Jesus Christ our Lord" (1:4). This formulation can be subject to misinterpretation, so it is important to get right what he is saying. Paul's point is that Jesus's resurrection reveals *who he was all along* (that is, God's Son and Messiah) in addition to signaling that he now reigns as Lord. Similarly, at the conclusion of the Christ hymn in Philippians, the exaltation of the Risen One in glory confirms "that Jesus Christ is Lord, / to the glory of God the Father" (Phil 2:9–11).

"Jesus is Lord" is the basic Christian confession of faith (cf. I Cor 12:3). Paul evokes this fundamental declaration in Romans when he announces, "If you confess with your lips that Jesus is Lord and believe in your heart that God raised him from the dead, you will be saved" (10:9). The Lordship of Jesus is universal and linked to Paul's insistence on the oneness of God. In I Corinthians

8:6, he sets forth a hymnic, creedal-like confession of the early Church: "There is one God, the Father, / from whom are all things and for whom we exist, / and one Lord, Jesus Christ, / through whom are all things and through whom we exist."[2] This passage is an adaptation of the *Shema*, the Jewish confession of faith ("Hear, O Israel: The LORD is our God, the LORD alone"; Deut 6:4). What is extraordinary about Paul's declaration in I Corinthians 8:6 is the way he brings Jesus as Lord into the oneness of God. Whereas God the Father is the source and goal of all creation, Jesus is the one through whom God creates and through whom God redeems (cf. Col 1:15–20). Passages like this were important in the development of the doctrine of the Trinity.

Whereas earlier in the Letter to the Romans, Paul asserted that "God is one," the God of both Jews and Gentiles, and that God saves both through the faithfulness of Jesus (3:29–30), he later declares—with reference to Jesus—that "the same Lord is Lord of all [of Jews and Gentiles] and is generous to all who call on him" (10:12). Once again, the Apostle brings the Lord Jesus within the ambit of monotheism. He goes on to appeal to the prophet Joel to give a scriptural basis to this claim: "Everyone who calls on the name of the Lord [Jesus] shall be saved" (10:13; cf. Joel 2:32). In their original context, Joel's words referred to YHWH. But now Paul applies them to Jesus as Lord. As we will see in the following section, the Scriptures are fulfilled in Christ.

As glorified Lord, Jesus shares in the divine prerogative at the final judgment: "On the day when, according to my gospel, God, through Jesus Christ, will judge the secret thoughts of all" (2:16; cf. Matt 25:31–46). In addition, Paul conveys another aspect of Jesus's heavenly Lordship, namely his role as intercessor. The Lord Jesus is "at the right hand of God" and "intercedes for us" (8:34; cf. Heb 9:24). The image of Jesus as our advocate before God is comforting, since he knows well the human condition (cf. 8:3). Likewise consoling is the knowledge that Jesus as Lord saves all who call upon his name. However, Jesus's Lordship also challenges us to refrain from judging others—only God has the right to judge (cf. 14:10–12)—and to ask ourselves constantly in what ways we are tempted to serve other "lords," whether it be concern for our reputation, the accumulation of possessions and status, the need for acceptance, and so on.

In addition to highlighting Jesus's present reign as Lord, Paul's Christology also implies both the preexistence of the Son and the incarnation. Admittedly, there is nothing in Romans to compare with the Prologue of John's Gospel, which declares that "the Word was with God" from the beginning (John 1:1), and that "the Word became flesh and lived among us" (John 1:14). Nevertheless, when Paul states that God "did not withhold his own Son, but gave him up for all of us" (8:32), he intimates that God *sent* the Son. And, of course, there had to be in existence a Son to send. This is more explicit in Galatians 4:4, where Paul writes, "But when the fullness of time had come, God sent his Son, born of a woman, born under the law." This is tantamount to a Pauline declaration of the incarnation.

In addition, the Christ hymn in Philippians contains a brief description of the pre-incarnate Christ: "Though he was in the form of God, / [he] did not regard equality with God / as something to be exploited, / but emptied himself, / taking the form of a slave, / being born in human likeness" (Phil 2:6–7). Observe the description of the Son's "equality with God." Yet he chose not to take advantage of that condition, but rather "emptied (*ekenōsen*) himself." What exactly this *kenosis* involved has long been debated. It is best understood to express all that is involved in one who is fully divine deciding to become human. The humble self-giving involved in the incarnation is replicated, as we saw in the previous section, in the obedience-unto-death of Jesus out of his love for humanity (Phil 2:8). Elsewhere, Paul captures succinctly both of these manifestations of self-giving love—incarnation and cross—in 2 Corinthians 8:9: "For you know the generous act of our Lord Jesus Christ, that though he was rich, yet for your sakes he became poor, so that by his poverty you might become rich."

JESUS THE FULFILLMENT OF SCRIPTURE

Another feature of Paul's Christology in Romans is how he understands Jesus vis-à-vis the Jewish Scriptures (what we today call the Old Testament). At the beginning of the letter, he states that God's gospel was "promised beforehand through his prophets in the holy scriptures" (1:2), a claim he reiterates in the concluding doxology (16:26). Moreover, as we saw in the previous chapter, Paul insists that Christ is the *telos nomou* (10:4)—the "end" or, better, the "goal" of the Law. There I argued that "law" refers more broadly to Torah, to the Jewish Scriptures (of which the first five books are known by Jews as "Torah"). This interpretation is bolstered by what Paul writes in 3:21, where he asserts that God's righteousness—revealed through the faithfulness of Christ—was "attested by the law and the prophets."[3] In the years following his encounter with the risen Lord, Paul reinterpreted the sacred texts he had known so well. He does so now in the light of the surprising way God has acted through a crucified (and risen) Messiah. He comes to appreciate that the One whom the Scriptures revealed as Creator and covenant God has fulfilled his promises to Israel (15:8; 2 Cor 1:20)—and by extension, to all peoples—through Jesus.

Paul explicitly links Jesus with Scripture in 15:3: "For Christ did not please himself; but, as it is written, 'The insults of those who insult you have fallen on me.'" This is the passage with which I began the introduction. The citation is from the Greek text of Psalm 69, a lament psalm that recounts the travails of one who suffers for his faithfulness to God, as well as his subsequent vindication by

God.[4] At the heart of Paul's citation is his conviction that Jesus's self-giving love, expressed in his passion, takes up and fulfills the pattern of the mysterious workings of God expressed in the psalm. Indeed, the early preaching of the Church turned to the Psalms to show that Jesus's passion, death, resurrection, and exaltation fulfilled what those texts proclaimed. A classic example is Peter's use of Psalms 16 and 110 in his speech following the spectacular outpouring of the Spirit at Pentecost (Acts 2:25–36).

Another suffering-and-vindicated biblical figure looms in the background of Paul's understanding of Jesus, the mysterious suffering servant portrayed in the Prophet Isaiah. The four so-called servant songs of Isaiah (Isa 42:1–7; 49:1–6; 50:4–9a; and 52:13—53:12) are read during the Church's Holy Week liturgies. In Romans, Paul draws on the fourth servant song, the song that most dramatically portrays the figure who, like a lamb led to slaughter, was as an offering for sin. His statement in 4:25 that Jesus "was handed over to death for our trespasses" alludes to Isaiah 53:5—"he was wounded for our transgressions" (cf. also Isa 53:10, 12). And his declaration in 5:19 that "by the one man's [Christ's] obedience the many will be made righteous" evokes Isaiah 53:11—"the righteous one, my servant, shall make many righteous."

We will return to the notion of Jesus as "the righteous one" in a moment. Paul makes another, more subtle use of the fourth Isaian servant song in 10:16. In the course of lamenting that not all (especially his fellow Jews) have received the gospel concerning God's Son with an open heart, he quotes Isaiah: "Lord, who has believed our message?" This line is from Isaiah 53:1, near the beginning of the fourth song. Paul's citation alludes to the entire song, which he reads as a prophetic foretelling of Jesus, the suffering Messiah. A suffering Christ, especially one who was put to death on a cross, defied all messianic expectations in the first century (cf., e.g., Mark 8:31–33; I Cor 1:18, 22). The Apostle evokes the Isaian servant in 10:16 in order to make the point that Israel's Scriptures do indicate that God's servant must suffer and die.

Paul's evocation of the Isaian servant in 10:16 follows immediately upon another quotation from the Prophet: "How beautiful are the feet of those who bring good news!" (10:15; cf. Isa 52:7). What is striking here is that the Apostle views himself, as well as other missionaries who proclaim the gospel, as fulfilling the Scriptures. This is an important point for Christians to consider. The story of Scripture—climaxing in the life, death, and resurrection of Jesus—*is to continue* in and through the life of the Church (e.g., in carrying out his ministry of teaching, feeding, and healing). Paul makes another allusion to Isaiah in connection with Jesus in 11:26–27: "'Out of Zion will come the Deliverer; / he will banish ungodliness from Jacob.' / 'And this is my covenant with them, / when I take away their sins'" (cf. Isa 59:20–21; 27:9). Commentators debate whether he employs this text in connection with what Jesus in his faithfulness has already accomplished, or points to the future when the risen Lord will return in glory (that is, from the heavenly Zion). The future tense verb ("will come") could indicate the second possibility.

As important as Isaiah is for Paul's portrayal of Jesus, the very first prophet he cites in Romans is Habakkuk. In 1:17—which constitutes the "thesis statement" of the letter—he writes in schematic fashion: "For in it [the gospel] the righteousness of God is revealed through faith for faith; as it is written, 'The righteous one (*ho dikaios*) will live by faith'" (au. trans.). The quoted passage, Habakkuk 2:4, is the first prophetic text following Paul's statement in 1:2 that the gospel was promised beforehand in the prophetic writings. This datum strongly suggests that he reads the Habakkuk passage as referring to Christ. *Jesus* is "the Righteous One" (cf. Acts 3:14; 7:52; 22:14) who now lives the fullness of resurrection life because of his faithfulness to God. Jesus could reveal God's righteousness because he himself is righteous, the quality expressed most eloquently in his self-donating love on the cross.

Paul refers to Christ's "act of righteousness" (*dikaiōma*) in the context of another biblical allusion, the comparison in 5:15–19 of Jesus to Adam. Adam's disobedience (cf. Gen 3) unleashed the cosmic powers of sin and death that then entrapped those who followed in his rebellion against God and his ways (5:12). But while the consequences of Adam's disobedience were disastrous, God's power now prevails through Jesus's obedience-unto-death. Through the Messiah's self-giving love, God has brought about "the abundance of grace and the free gift of righteousness" (5:17)—in short, the possibility of the fullness of life, including transformation into the likeness of "the Righteous One." As Paul states, "By the one man's obedience the many will be made righteous" (5:19).

Twice in this chapter, we have noted the Christ hymn in Philippians 2:6–11. The first three verses, making up the first half of the hymn, depict Jesus against the foil of the story of Adam.[5] Whereas Adam, created in the image of God (Gen 1:26), grasped after life where it was not offered to him (Gen 3:6), the Son, who was in "the form of God," did not exploit his divine status. Whereas Adam's motivation was to exalt himself (cf. Gen 3:5—"you will be like God"), Jesus's modus operandi was guided by humility, by his lowering himself and taking the "form of a slave." And whereas Adam's defining characteristic was disobedience, Jesus's life trajectory was marked by obedience, even "to the point of death." The first half of the hymn therefore manifests another way Jesus fulfills the Scriptures, here as reversing what Adam launched through his disobedience.

JESUS THE NEW ADAM

Paul's comparison of Jesus to Adam implies that Jesus is the new or second Adam. His use of Adam as a foil for understanding Jesus is multifaceted. In 1 Corinthians 15, Paul focuses on what

Jesus's resurrection reveals with reference to Adam. Adam is the "human being" (*anthrōpos*) through whom death entered the world; but now the resurrection of the dead has come through another *anthrōpos*, Christ (1 Cor 15:21). And this has implications for all of humanity: "For as all die in Adam, so all will be made alive in Christ" (1 Cor 15:22). That is, the risen Jesus is the "first fruits" of those whom God will raise from the dead on the last day. While the first Adam "became a living being," the second Adam "became a life-giving spirit," the one through whom God's Spirit—over whom death has no power—is bestowed (1 Cor 15:45).

The Adam-Christ comparison in Romans, as we have seen, focuses on the issue of obedience. Paul's emphasis shades here into what Jesus teaches about being truly human. On the one hand, as God's Son and the Messiah, Jesus reveals who God is and enacts the divine plan of salvation; as Pope Francis beautifully expresses it: "Jesus Christ is the face of the Father's Mercy" (MV 1, 24). On the other hand, as the new Adam, Jesus shows forth authentic human existence. Through his life, death, and resurrection, Jesus has restored the possibility of enacting the basic human vocation, namely to grow into that which we are created to be: the image of God (*eikōn theou*). But what precisely does this mean?

While Paul considered Adam to be a historical person, he also (and more importantly) regarded him as a representative figure, one who stands at the head of the old humanity—what he calls, literally, the "old *anthrōpos*" (Col 3:9). This way of being is marked by rejection of God and his ways, self-seeking, covetousness, vengefulness, and the total breakdown of relationships (1:29–31). But Jesus, as the "image of God" par excellence (cf. 2 Cor 4:4), reveals another way of being human: faithfully loving God and being obedient to his will, being grateful, seeking the advantage of others, being willing to forgive—in short, the way of self-giving love. Jesus stands at the head of a renewed humanity, the "new *anthrōpos*" (Col 3:10), having ushered in the new creation (2 Cor 5:17; Gal 6:15).

To be an "image of God" is to reflect something of the glory of God to others. And Jesus shows that the essence of God is love. The Greek word for "image," *eikōn*, is the source of our word *icon*. Religious icons have many purposes, one of which is to be, in effect, a "window" through which we glimpse spiritual realities. To be an "icon of God" is to live in such a way that others can look at me and glimpse the God of love whose Spirit—"the Spirit of Christ" (8:9)—indwells and empowers me. This is an awesome vocation, one that underlies the more particular callings God gives. In emphasizing the importance of obedience to God and his will, Paul insists on the necessity for prayerful discernment (12:2). Happily, he also teaches that the Spirit assists us by interceding to God for us according to his will (8:27). We can now appreciate even more the Apostle's passion for helping to bring about the "obedience of faith" (1:5; 16:26).

In the closing exhortations in Romans (12:1—15:13), Paul gives further texture to the way of being human as revealed by Jesus, the new Adam. He does so in two ways. First, Paul exhorts the believers in Rome to "put on the Lord Jesus Christ" (13:14). To "put on" Jesus is to take on and appropriate those qualities and characteristics that distinguished him. Paul subtly weaves a number of these characteristics into his exposition. For example, he encourages the believers in Rome to "pursue what makes for peace and for mutual upbuilding" (14:19). What is meant here is living with keen sensitivity to the needs of others, always striving for what edifies rather than tears down. This also entails bearing with the weaknesses of others, while being committed to do what is best for them (15:1–2). Such exhortations are given greater contour and shape when one recalls those moments in Jesus's ministry that highlight his compassion (e.g., Mark 6:34).

Correspondingly, Paul prays that God will enable the Romans "to think the same among yourselves according to Messiah Jesus" (15:5, au. trans.). The wording here (including the verb for "think," *phroneō*) is similar to the exhortation that introduces the Christ hymn in Philippians 2:5. As we have seen, that hymn sets forth, among other things, Jesus's servant ministry (cf. 15:8; Mark 10:45), one that reflects his mindset. To offer oneself in loving service to others, after the manner of Jesus, is to walk in the way of love (14:15). So, too, is heeding Paul's command to "welcome one another... just as Christ has welcomed you" (15:7). This evokes Jesus's openness to all as expressed, for instance, by his table fellowship (e.g., Luke 5:30–32). This exhortation to extend mutual hospitality was necessary for the diverse membership—Jews and Gentiles, rich and poor—of the Roman house churches (cf. 16:3–16). It is no less so in communities today.

The second way in which Paul offers texture to "new Adam existence" is by recalling some crucial elements of Jesus's teaching. Like Jesus, Paul sums up the commandments of the Jewish Law—at least those pertaining to relations with other people—by citing Leviticus 19:18: "Love your neighbor as yourself" (13:9; cf. Matt 22:39). Even more striking is the way he echoes Jesus's instructions from the Sermon on the Mount. Paul admonishes the faithful in Rome not to be overcome by evil, but rather to "overcome evil with good" (12:21), which harkens back to Jesus's commands against retaliation (Matt 5:38–42—"You have heard that it was said, 'An eye for an eye and a tooth for a tooth.' But I say to you, Do not resist an evildoer."). Moreover, he exhorts the Romans, "Bless those who persecute you; bless and do not curse them" (12:14), which recalls Jesus's most radical command: to love one's enemies (Matt 5:43–48).

The rationale behind Jesus's command to love one's enemies is important to appreciate. He says that in widening the scope of the recipients of our love—even to persecutors and to those who hate us—we show ourselves to be true children of the "Father in heaven," who sends sunshine and rain on the good and the bad alike (Matt 5:45). In other words, to cast wide the nets of our love is to take on the divine family resemblance, as it were. Paul makes a similar point in Romans via the image of Jesus as the new Adam. By clothing ourselves with his characteristics and by heeding his teaching, we are more and more "conformed to the image of [God's] Son, in order that he might be the firstborn within a large family" (8:29). To be conformed to the image of God's Son—who himself is the image of God par excellence—is to grow in manifesting the family likeness. And when groups or communities of the faithful do so, they become "one body in Christ" (12:5; cf. I Cor 12:27), making him incarnate in space and time today.

Paul's Christology in Romans is remarkably rich and robust. Jesus is the Messiah and Son of God whose faithfulness/obedience-unto-death is the means by which God has revealed his righteousness and acted to defeat the powers of sin and death. Raised from the dead, Jesus reigns as Lord and intercedes for those who call upon his name. Jesus is the fulfillment of the Jewish Scriptures, the climax of the story of God's faithfulness to his covenant promises, the story of God's love and presence that is to continue in the life of the Church. As the new Adam, Jesus shows forth authentic human existence, lived in obedience to God and expressed through self-giving love. Such a life, however, is possible only because of the gift of the Spirit, the topic of the next chapter.

QUESTIONS FOR PRAYER AND REFLECTION

1. How does the interpretation of *pistis Christou* as "Christ's faithfulness" help me to appreciate his salvific mission? How can it impact my own sense of discipleship?

2. How does the realization that *Christos* means "anointed one" affect the way I think about the anointings I have received in the sacraments of baptism and confirmation?

3. When I consider the word *obedience*, what comes to mind? In what ways does Paul's presentation of Jesus's obedience challenge or encourage me? How am I being called to listen to God more intently?

4. What does the term *Lord* conjure? When I confess in the Nicene Creed that "I believe in one Lord Jesus Christ," what am I saying, and to what am I committing myself?

5. How often do I consider that Jesus the Lord is interceding on my behalf to the Father? How might this help my trusting that God is really "for us"?

6. Paul's experience of the risen Lord was dramatic, leading him to reread the Scriptures. In what ways have my eyes been opened to read the Scriptures with fresh comprehension?

7. What do I make of Paul's understanding his missionary activity as fulfilling the word of Scripture? How might I be motivated to see myself—and my faith community—as continuing the story of God's love in the world?

8. How does Paul's presentation of Jesus as the new Adam help me to think about what it means to be truly human?

9. Who have been "icons" of God for me? How might I be called to be a more faithful "icon" of God?

10. What do I find inspiring or challenging about the ways Paul, in his exhortations to the Romans, draws on the teaching and character of Jesus?

3

SPIRIT

[Jesus] was declared to be Son of God with power according to the Spirit of holiness by resurrection from the dead.

— Romans 1:4; NRSV alt. trans.

May the God of hope fill you with all joy and peace in believing, so that you may abound in hope by the power of the Holy Spirit.

— Romans 15:13

The doctrine of the Trinity—the mystery that God is one in three Persons—took until the late fourth century to be fully developed. It would therefore be historically anachronistic to read later trinitarian doctrine back onto Paul. Nevertheless, it can rightly be said that what would come to be articulated in more metaphysical terminology extrapolates, in large part, what is found in his letters. And, in terms of pneumatology (that is, the understanding of the Spirit of God, from the Greek *pneuma*—"spirit," "breath," "wind"), there is no letter more important than Romans. In fact, chapter 8 contains the most sustained treatment of the Holy Spirit in the entire New Testament.

Another manifestation of the importance of the Spirit in Romans is the fact that Paul highlights the "Spirit of holiness" in the opening lines of the letter. The alternative rendering in the NRSV footnote rightly, in my opinion, capitalizes "Spirit" (1:4). There Paul refers to the divine Spirit in conjunction with the resurrection of Jesus, a linkage found throughout the New Testament (cf. John 20:19–23; Luke 24:36–49). That is, the resurrection of Jesus marks a turning point in history in which God pours forth the Spirit "on all flesh" (Joel 2:28; Acts 2:17). Moreover, in a prayer at the end of the body of the letter (15:13), Paul asks God to bestow joy, peace, and hope on the believers in Rome "by the power of the Holy Spirit." The gift of the Spirit is thus closely associated with resurrection power, manifested by joy and peace in the present and hope for the future.

These two passages point to several aspects of Paul's teaching about the Holy Spirit in the Letter to the Romans. First, however, it will be necessary to offer some preliminary remarks about certain biblical eschatological promises and the fluidity of the Apostle's terminology. With these introductory observations in place, we can then explore what Paul says about the Spirit vis-à-vis baptism; what he means when he refers to the Spirit as the "Spirit of adoption"; and how he understands the conforming/transforming power of the Spirit.

PRELIMINARY REMARKS

A striking feature when reading the New Testament is how dramatically the early Church experienced the outpouring of God's Spirit. But what often goes unnoticed is how members of the early Church *interpreted* that experience. They were completely convinced that it fulfilled certain well-known eschatological (that is, looking to the end time) promises, many of which were contained in the prophetic writings. Paul alludes to two such passages in 2 Corinthians 3:2–3. In response to criticism that, unlike other missionaries, he did not carry with him letters of recommendation, he informs the Corinthian community, "You yourselves are our letter, written on our hearts, to be known and read by all; and you show that you are a letter of Christ, prepared by us, written not with ink but with the Spirit of the living God, not on tablets of stone but on tablets of fleshy hearts" (au. trans.).

Paul's metaphor here is complex. For our purposes, it is sufficient to focus on the two prophetic passages that provide much of the imagery he employs in these verses. The references to "the Spirit of the living God" and to "fleshy hearts"—soft, malleable ones, in contrast to hard, stony ones—evoke Ezekiel 36:26–27, where the prophet declares on God's behalf: "A new heart I will give you, and a new spirit I will put within you; and I will remove from your body the heart of stone and give you *a heart of flesh. I will put my spirit within you*, and make you follow my statutes and be careful to observe my ordinances" (cf. Ezek 11:19, au. emphasis). Notice how Ezekiel uses the imagery of a heart transplant God will perform on his people. He also reports that God will pour out his life-giving Spirit on them. These words were spoken in the context of the promise to God's people that they would return from exile. However, they came to express Israel's hopes for what God would do *in the future*, on the day when he would definitively intervene on his people's behalf.

Similarly, the phrase "written on our hearts" (2 Cor 3:2) recalls Jeremiah 31:33: "But this is the covenant that I will make with the house of Israel after those days, says the LORD: I will put my law within them, and *I will write it on their hearts*; and I will be their God, and they shall be my people" (au. emphasis). Here God assures his people that he will establish a "new covenant" (Jer 31:31)—the only time this phrase is used in the Old Testament. This covenant will be marked by a profound interiorizing. That is, Jeremiah prophesies that there will come a time when God not only places his Law within his people, but also bestows on them the wherewithal to carry it out in order that they can be his holy people.

Paul came to appreciate that the outpouring of the divine Spirit on the members of the Church, following the death and resurrection of Jesus, is the very fulfillment of these prophetic promises. Through Christ, the covenant God has *already* intervened on behalf of his people—indeed, on behalf of "all" (cf. 2 Cor 5:14–15), including the whole of creation. The gift of the Spirit is truly a "game changer." These prophetic texts are also in the background when Paul speaks in Romans of a circumcision that "is a matter of the heart," one that is spiritual and now enables the recipients of the Spirit to keep God's Law (2:25–29), and when he later remarks that the Spirit's empowerment is such that "the just requirement of the law might be fulfilled in us" (8:4). This "just requirement"—as we saw in chapter 2—can be summarized as self-giving love, which is the fulfillment of God's Law (13:9–10).

Paul is therefore utterly sanguine about the unleashing of God's power through the Spirit *in the here and now*. The contemporary Church has much to learn from this conviction about the Spirit's presence and influence. Those who have been baptized and confirmed have received the very same Spirit whose dynamic force is described throughout the New Testament—not least in the Acts of the Apostles. Yet, truth be told, we do not seem to experience the "demonstration of the Spirit and of power" that should accompany the proclamation of the gospel (cf. 1 Cor 2:4). Nor do we encounter other dramatic manifestations of the Spirit, such as healings. Might it be that we are not opening ourselves fully to the power of the Spirit of God? How often do I pray explicitly to the Spirit for his[1] help and assistance? As we will discover, the Apostle offers much to reflect on how we can deepen our sense of the Spirit's presence and strength.

Another preliminary point concerns Paul's terminology with reference to the Spirit. His terminology is marked by fluidity, as illustrated by Romans 8:9: "You are in the Spirit, since the Spirit of God dwells in you. Anyone who does not have the Spirit of Christ does not belong to him." Observe how, within a single verse, he mentions the "Spirit," the "Spirit of God," and the "Spirit of Christ." Now, without a doubt, the referent of all three phrases is one and the same—namely, *God's* Spirit. By the "Spirit of Christ," Paul signifies the divine Spirit that animated Jesus during his earthly life and ministry (cf. Luke 4:16–21). This is the same Spirit through whom God raised him from the dead: "If the Spirit of him [God] who raised Jesus from the dead dwells in you, he who raised Christ from the dead will give life to your mortal bodies also through his Spirit that dwells in you" (8:11).

Paul can also talk in the same passage about being "in the Spirit" (8:9) on the one hand, and, on the other hand, about the Spirit's indwelling people (8:9, 11). What does it mean to be "in the Spirit"? The gift of the Spirit brings his recipients (every instance of the pronoun "you" in 8:9–11 is plural) into a sacred "sphere" that unites them to other members, demarcates them as a community of faith, and protects them from the forces of sin and evil. This is an aspect of "the *koinōnia* of the Holy Spirit" (2 Cor 13:13), the "fellowship" or "communion" the Spirit brings about among the faithful in creating manifestations of the "body of Christ" (cf. 1 Cor 12:13). A very important implication is that this body's sanctity—note, the gathering Spirit is the *Holy* Spirit—must be carefully safeguarded (cf. 1 Cor 5:1–5).

What, then, does it mean for Paul to say that "the Spirit of God dwells in you" (8:9)? This indicates the Spirit's taking residence (recall the sense of the verb *oikeō*) within the core of each and every member of the Body of Christ. Paul calls this core of one's being the "heart" (*kardia*). It is through the mediation of the indwelling Spirit that he can remind the believers in Rome that "Christ is in you" (8:10). And it is because of the Holy Spirit's indwelling embodied individuals that Paul can ask the Corinthians, "Do you not know that your body is a temple[2] of the Holy Spirit within you, which you have from God?" (I Cor 6:19). This is a mystery worth reflecting on. Paul's use of temple imagery is a reminder of the dignity each of us has as a dwelling place of the Spirit. The proper response to this gift is to "glorify God in your body" (I Cor 6:20; cf. Rom 12:1). I am to treasure myself as one in whom God deigns to dwell, and to honor the divine presence in others. As an embodied being inhabited by God's Spirit, it matters deeply what I do to and with my body—as well as to and with the bodies of others.

THE SPIRIT AND BAPTISM

Paul refers to the indwelling Spirit when he declares in 5:5 that "God's love has been poured into our hearts through the Holy Spirit that has been given to us." "Pouring" evokes the image of water, with its cleansing and life-giving properties. Although Paul does not explicitly mention baptism here, it is implied. The verb "poured" is in the perfect tense, which we have seen signifies an action in the past that has lasting consequences. Baptism effects the personal reception of God's love—the love revealed in God's sending his only Son (8:32), the same love manifested in Jesus's death on the cross (5:8; 8:35). And this gift of divine love *perdures*, as the Spirit takes up residence with us. Whereas Jesus, through his incarnation and birth, is "God-with-us" (the meaning of Emmanuel; cf. Matt 1:23), the indwelling Spirit is God-*within*-us—that is, within each individual Christian and within the community of believers as a whole.

Paul goes on to offer an extended reflection on baptism in 6:3–11 that sheds light on what happens when the gift of the Spirit is bestowed and received. One striking feature is the way he emphasizes its dynamic quality. Those who are baptized are "baptized *into* (the preposition is *eis*, not *en* ["in"]) Christ Jesus." At one level, this means, as Paul declares elsewhere, that "in the one Spirit we were all baptized into one body" (1 Cor 12:13), that is, into the community of faith, the Body of Christ. This intimate connection between Jesus and the community of his followers was likely planted in the Apostle's mind when, in the course of pursuing Christ-believers, he was met by the Risen One, who asked, "Saul, Saul, why do you persecute *me*?" (Acts 9:4, au. emphasis).[3]

At another level, baptism effects intimate personal union with Jesus. More specifically, it brings about participation in Jesus's death. Paul points to this participation by using a number of verbs that begin with the preposition *syn* ("with," a prefix that carries over into English words like *sympathize*, which means "to feel with"). Those who are baptized are even "buried with" Christ (6:4), likely an allusion to the full immersion into the baptismal waters. Because they are associated with Christ in his death and burial, the baptized have truly "died" in the sense that they have "died to sin," to the ways that lead to spiritual death (6:2).

The gift of the Spirit bestowed in baptism also involves participation in the resurrection of Jesus. Because he was raised from the dead by the Spirit of God (8:11)—who is the Spirit of life— "death no longer has dominion over him [Jesus]" (6:9). Those who are baptized into Jesus's death are also raised into new life through the same Spirit. This new life has a twofold dimension. Here we arrive at Paul's "already-but-not-yet" understanding of resurrection life. In terms of the "not yet": those who are united with Christ in death "will certainly be united with him in a resurrection like his" (6:5; cf. 8:11). Observe the future tense of the verb. Paul refers here to the future, general resurrection of the dead (cf. 1 Thess

4:13–18), of which Christ is the "first fruits" (1 Cor 15:20–28). Elsewhere, he describes the Spirit as an *arrabōn*, translated by the NRSV as a "first installment" (2 Cor 1:22), a "guarantee" (2 Cor 5:5), and "pledge" (Eph 1:14) of our future inheritance—the fullness of resurrection life.

In terms of the "already": the Spirit also brings about resurrection life in the here and now. Indeed, before the statement about the future resurrection in 6:5, Paul declares that "just as Christ was raised from the dead by the glory of the Father, so we too might walk in newness of life" (6:4). The image of walking conveys daily behavior and conduct. Having died to sin—with its various manifestations of self-seeking—those who are baptized can live for God and for others. This "here and now" aspect of resurrection life is something on which Paul constantly insists in all his letters. Once again, he is extremely confident in the present manifestation of the Spirit's empowerment. We sell ourselves short when we fail to appropriate the force of the "already" aspect of resurrection life.

In the following sections, we will look more closely at how Paul understands Spirit-empowered "newness of life." However, it is here worth mentioning another feature of his baptismal teaching that will foreshadow that treatment. Paul exhorts the Romans to "put on the Lord Jesus Christ" (13:14). He can do so because they have *already* put on Christ when they were baptized. Indeed, in Galatians 3:27, he proclaims, "As many of you as were baptized into Christ have clothed yourselves with Christ." Although the exact details of how baptism was celebrated in the early Church, including during Paul's ministry, are not available to us, it is possible that the baptized put on new clothes to symbolize the new people they had become (a practice that was to become the case). The exhortation to put on Christ means to take on and appropriate, more and more, the teachings and characteristics—in short, the self-giving love—of Jesus. The "Spirit of Christ" (8:9) empowers this maturation, which allows people to be "all dressed up" in the best sense of that phrase.

Another passage that illuminates what happens when people receive the Spirit is 2 Corinthians 1:21–22. There Paul describes something God has done for him and his fellow ministers: "It is God who…has anointed us, by putting his seal on us and giving us his Spirit in our hearts as a first installment." To be sure, this passage does not refer explicitly to baptism. However, given what the Apostle goes on to teach in the rest of the letter (see, e.g., 2 Cor 3:17–18; 5:5), what is depicted here is something that in fact has happened to *all* who are now in Christ. And that "something" occurred with both reception of the gospel message and baptism.

Paul associates two vivid images with the bestowal of the Spirit: anointing and putting on a seal. The verb "anoint" is *chriō*, from which is derived the words "Christ" (that is, "Messiah" = "anointed one") and "chrism," the name of the sacred oil for anointings (used in the Catholic sacraments of baptism, confirmation, and ordination). This verb appears only four other times in the entire New Testament, all in connection with Jesus (Luke 4:18; Acts 4:27; 10:38; and Heb 1:9). In Luke 4:18–21, Jesus announces that his anointing—"The Spirit of the Lord is upon me, / because he has anointed me"—was for the purpose of his bringing good news to the poor, giving sight to the blind, freeing the oppressed, and proclaiming God's favor. This suggests an understanding of what it means, literally, to be "christed" (2 Cor 1:21): the baptized are called and enabled to participate in Jesus's ministry. It is no coincidence that, in the Rite for Baptism, immediately following the baptism proper comes the anointing with chrism, at which is prayed, "As Christ was anointed Priest, Prophet, and King, so may you live always as a member of his body."

Paul's second vivid image is being sealed (cf. Eph 1:13—"In [Christ] you also, when you had heard the word of truth, the gospel of your salvation, and had believed in him, were marked with the seal of the promised Holy Spirit"). The verb "seal" (*sphragizō*) can denote putting a mark on something in order to indicate possession. For instance, library books bear a mark or seal. To be sealed with the Spirit at baptism means that one belongs to God as a member of his holy people, and that one enjoys his loving protection and care (cf. Rev 9:4). This is Paul's primary meaning. In addition, "seal" can refer to the act of impressing an image onto something. For instance, a signet ring can be pressed into hot wax to make an impression for the purpose of authenticating a document (cf. 1 Kgs 21:8). Does Paul intend this added connotation? As we will see in the final section, the Spirit "conforms" and "transforms" his recipients into the image of Christ. Through the seal of the Spirit at baptism, God both marks people as his own and "impresses" on them the likeness of Christ.

THE SPIRIT OF ADOPTION AND WALKING IN THE SPIRIT

Knowing one's identity is a fundamental human need. It is a *sine qua non* (essential condition) for personal well-being, for appreciating one's sense of dignity, and for motivating one's decisions, including life choices. The most important identity marker we have, conferred through the gift of the Spirit at baptism, is adoption as God's children. In 8:14–15, Paul highlights this identity as follows: "All who are led by the Spirit of God are sons of God (*huioi theou*)....you have received the Spirit of adoption (*pneuma huiothesias*)" (au. trans.). My translation differs from the NRSV in two key respects. First, the phrase "spirit of adoption" (NRSV) is a reference to the divine Spirit through whom God adopts. Second, I render the phrase *huioi theou* literally as "sons of God" for reasons that we will now discuss.

Adoption (*huiothesia*) was rather common in the Greco-Roman world. It created a relationship of kinship recognized as equal to the relationship involved in natural descent. The word *huiothesia*—literally, "placing of the son"—denotes the establishment of a father-son relationship, a true belonging to the family with the rights and privileges contained therein, including the adopted son becoming an heir. Jewish tradition used the notion of adoption as a metaphor to describe the relationship between God and Israel (9:4; cf. Jer 31:9, where God announces, "I have become a father to Israel, / and Ephraim is my firstborn"), and the relationship between God and the king (2 Sam 7:14, with the adoption formula "I will be a father to him, and he shall be a son to me"; cf. Ps 2:7).

Paul uses the metaphor of adoption to describe what God has done through the death and resurrection of Jesus and the conferral of the Spirit. I have retained "sons" (masculine) in the translation in order to convey, at one level, the cultural reality that it was typically males, and not females, who were adopted. At a deeper and more important level, "sons" (*huioi*) indicates that the identity of the baptized is closely connected with Jesus, the "Son of God" (1:4). As some of the early Church fathers taught, what Jesus is by nature, the baptized are by adoption. Having made this observation, it is crucial to point out that Paul immediately clarifies in 8:16 that *both* males and females become God's "children," his sons and daughters, by virtue of their baptism (cf. 2 Cor 6:18). He does so by using the more inclusive term *tekna*.

The close connection with Jesus is indicated by two more textual clues. First, Paul states that the Spirit inspires his recipients to call out to God as "Abba," the same term Jesus employed when addressing his Father in prayer (8:15; cf. Mark 14:36). It connotes an intimate relationship and reveals God to be like a tender, loving parent, always there for his beloved children. This image of God—so decisive for a healthy spiritual life—is inculcated in a special way in the love parents have for their children. As Pope

Francis points outs, both individually and in their mutual love for one another, parents can show forth to their children the paternal and maternal face of God. This, of course, is an awesome privilege and responsibility. Grandparents, too, have the opportunity to reflect this intimate love of God.

The second textual clue is Paul's contrast of "the Spirit of adoption" with "a spirit of slavery to fall back into fear." *Phobos* here signifies the fear of death that often compels people to seek after what they think will be life-giving but ultimately is not, because true life is given only by God (cf. Heb 2:14–15). At the risk of oversimplifying, the impetus behind people trying to fill themselves in unhealthy ways—whether with food, drink, drugs, sex, possessions—is the realization that they are mortal. The tragic thing is that this quest for "life" leads away from God, who is the Creator and Source of all life. Of course, there is a salutary fear in the spiritual life, the "fear of the Lord." This refers to the reverent awe with which we are called to stand before God the Father; this awe also entails loving trust in God. It is this loving trust that Jesus embodied in his obedience-unto-death (5:19; Phil 2:8).

Another way Paul depicts the contrast between two ways of being is when he discusses setting one's mind on "the things of the Spirit" rather than on "the things of the flesh" (8:5). Here we encounter his famous distinction between the Spirit and the flesh (8:5–8; Gal 5:16–26). But it is imperative to get right what Paul means by "flesh" (*sarx*) in this regard. At times, he employs *sarx* in a descriptive sense in order to express the reality that human beings are incarnate, that is, made of flesh. Earlier in this chapter, we encountered the reference to "fleshy hearts" (2 Cor 3:3; au. trans. of *kardia sarkina*). Another example of this descriptive use of *sarx* is Galatians 2:20, where Paul writes, "Christ lives in me. And the life I now live in the flesh I live by the faithfulness of the Son of God,[4] who loved me and gave himself for me" (au. trans.). Using *sarx* in this sense, he affirms the goodness of embodied human existence.

When Paul contrasts the flesh with the Spirit, however, he operates with a different—and more theological—understanding of *sarx*. This sense of "flesh" indicates human existence after the manner of the first Adam, the "old *anthrōpos*" (Col 3:9), that is not only subject to physical corruption but also rebellious against God and his ways. Paul asserts that "the mind that is set on the flesh is hostile to God; it does not submit to God's law—indeed, it cannot" (8:7). *Sarx* in this technical sense is completely opposed to the Spirit. In Galatians 5:19–21, Paul details the "works of the flesh"—the products of such living—as "fornication, impurity, licentiousness, idolatry, sorcery, enmities, strife, jealousy, anger, quarrels, dissensions, factions, envy, drunkenness, carousing, and things like these." A common denominator in this catalog of vices is the consequent breakdown of relationships and community.

To be in the Spirit is to live as embodied human beings who are enabled to conduct themselves (recall the image of "walking" referred to above) in a diametrically opposite manner. Immediately following this vice catalog, Paul offers a list of the "fruit" (*karpos*) of the Spirit: "love, joy, peace, patience, kindness, generosity, faithfulness, gentleness, and self-control" (Gal 5:22–23). It is important to emphasize that he describes these as "fruit" (singular). This is not a list from which one can pick and choose two or three qualities one likes or is good at. No, to set one's mind on the things of the Spirit is to grow in all nine characteristics. I will return to the Apostle's use of virtue lists in the following section.

But first, Paul concludes his paragraph on the metaphor of adoption in Romans by stating that the Spirit not only bears witness that his recipients are God's children (8:16). They are also *heirs*—and more specifically, "joint heirs with Christ" (8:17). The inheritance is the fullness of resurrection life, which Jesus already enjoys. But the path to this inheritance is, like the one he trod, the path of suffering. Paul refers here to the sacrifice entailed in loving and serving others, as well as to the opposition that commitment to the gospel can provoke in those who reject it. The Spirit bestows the wherewithal to endure all suffering. Paul asserts that "suffering produces endurance, and endurance produces character, and character produces hope" (5:3–4). Indeed, a distinguishing mark of the Spirit's presence and power is that it allows his recipients to "abound in hope" (15:13). The witness value of Christian hope should never be underestimated—especially in today's world.

THE SPIRIT AND CONFORMATION/ TRANSFORMATION

In addition to assisting people in their suffering, Paul teaches that the Spirit "helps us in our weakness," at those times when it is hard to pray, perhaps because hope seems so difficult. At such times, the Spirit "intercedes [for us] with sighs too deep for words" (8:26). The Spirit is not only God-within-us, but also God-*for*-us, advocating on our behalf in ways we could never do for ourselves. The indwelling Spirit is closer to us than we are to ourselves; the Spirit knows us better than we know ourselves. And God the Father, the one who searches hearts (cf. Ps 139), understands and responds to the Spirit's groaning on behalf of his children. That is because the Spirit intercedes "according to the will of God" (8:27).

The reference to God's will leads naturally to the Spirit's role in empowering people to live after the manner of Jesus, the new Adam, whose entire life was characterized by fidelity (3:22) and obedience (5:19) to the will of his heavenly Father—even to the point of offering his life in love on the cross. In 8:29, Paul alludes to the Spirit's work of *conforming* (cf. the adjective *symmorphos*) people to "the image of [God's] Son," the "firstborn" among many brothers and sisters. That is, the Spirit labors to enable his recipients to take on the likeness of God's family. As noted earlier, one way the

Spirit does so is by instilling loving trust in God as the source and sustainer of life.

Paul offers further explanation of the Spirit's work in 12:2, where he exhorts the faithful in Rome to "be transformed by the renewing of your minds, so that you may discern what is the will of God." The verb "transform" is *metamorphoō*, from which we get "metamorphosis." Paul employs the passive voice of the verb, thereby indicating divine agency. In 2 Corinthians 3:18, he names the Spirit as that agent of transformation (again using the verb *metamorphoō*). It is no surprise that there he describes the Spirit as transforming people into "the same image"—that is, into the likeness of Jesus, the "image of God" par excellence (2 Cor 4:4).[5] The Spirit-driven renewal of people's minds involves their being helped to have a new mindset, to think first and foremost of the things of God (8:5–8). It entails, as Paul describes in 1 Corinthians 2:16, the bestowal of the "mind of Christ" (*nous Christou*), the inculcation of Jesus's fundamental attitudes, values, qualities, and ways of looking at and treating others.

The final section of the previous chapter (on Jesus the new Adam) anticipated some of this discussion of the conforming/transforming power of the Spirit. Another way of getting at this point is to look at the virtue lists in Paul's letters. These lists provide, in effect, "word portraits" of Jesus. The qualities that Paul calls his communities to "put on"—with the Spirit's assistance and guidance—are those Jesus embodied in his life and ministry. One such list is Galatians 5:22–23, to which we referred earlier when discussing the contrast between Spirit and flesh. At the head of the list is "love" (*agapē*), the commitment to seek always what is good and truly life-giving for others. Jesus manifests the full extent of love in his self-offering on the cross (5:6–8; cf. Eph 5:2; John 15:13). For the Apostle, such love for others is an essential expression of one's love for and "faithfulness" (*pistis*, the seventh quality listed) to God. "Joy" and "peace," prominently listed after "love," then mark those who embody this faithfulness and love.

Paul's teaching here gives reason to pause. Many people today go to great lengths to pursue happiness and peace. The irony is that this sort of pursuit has things backward. Peace and joy are not commodities that can be bought or things that can be found. Rather, they "find" us when we are growing into the people God calls us to be. Understood in this way, joy and peace are not ephemeral experiences, subject to the vagaries of circumstances and emotion, but deep-seated gifts—bestowed by the Spirit (15:13)—that allow us to navigate the exigencies of life with the equanimity of knowing we are loved by God as his beloved children.

The other five qualities of the "fruit" of the conforming/transforming Spirit are practical expressions of saying yes to the process of maturation into God's image. "Patience" allows others the time and the space—as well as the encouragement—so that they may grow. It renders to them the compassion Jesus extended throughout his ministry (e.g., Mark 6:34; cf. Col 3:12). "Kindness" involves attention to the little things that make all the difference—a smile, a word of support, a check to see how others are doing. "Goodness" consists in that radiant expression of the integrity the Spirit helps to achieve in people. "Gentleness" enacts the loving manner with which Jesus met and treated others; hence, those who are in the Spirit should be true gentlemen and gentlewomen. "Self-control" summons the discipline and the perseverance necessary to grow in the way of holiness revealed by the new Adam.

First Corinthians 13:4–7 ("Love is patient; love is kind....") provides another such list of attributes empowered by the conforming/transforming Spirit. This passage, the middle of Paul's famous encomium on love—the "more excellent way" (1 Cor 12:31)—is the subject of a moving homiletic reflection by Pope Francis in *Amoris Laetitia*. For our purposes, I limit myself to two observations. First, if one removes the word "love" and all the instances of "it" (which refer to "love"), and then replaces them with the name "Jesus," there results a beautiful expression of how the latter conducted himself in his life and ministry. Doing so gives texture and contour to the love the Apostle calls for in this passage.

Second, the typical English translation of I Corinthians 13:4–7 does not convey an important grammatical point embedded in Paul's exposition. The NRSV can give the impression that the linking verb "is" predominates, especially in verses 4–5. But all of Paul's verbs in this passage are *action* verbs. While a bit awkward, a better (and more literal) way to express his meaning is "Love practices acts of patience and enacts kindness...." The crucial point is that, for Paul, love is not just a noun; it is also a verb, an action verb at that. To grow in the likeness of Jesus entails "practicing" the ways the conforming/transforming Spirit enables one to live. Therefore, when Paul exhorts the believers in Rome to be "aglow with the Spirit" (12:11 RSV), he means to be on fire with "the love of the Spirit" (15:30), the Spirit of Christ. As much as our world needs the witness of hope, it needs even more the fire of this love.

The Letter to the Romans is, to say the least, an essential source for understanding Paul's pneumatology. His (and the early Church's) experience of the Spirit's power led him to conclude that it fulfilled the prophecies concerning God's promises to create new hearts and fill them with his Spirit. The gift of the Spirit, conferred at baptism, both creates a new identity and inspires a new way of life. We who are baptized are adopted as God's children. Moreover, we are in the process of being conformed and transformed more and more into the likeness of Jesus and his manner of self-giving love. In short, Paul has a strong appreciation of *sanctification*, of being made holy by God's Spirit. In the next chapter, we will look at other facets of God's saving action.

QUESTIONS FOR PRAYER AND REFLECTION

1. When have I witnessed or experienced the power of the Holy Spirit at work in me? In others? What were the manifestations of this power?

2. How can Paul's image of individuals and communities as temples of the Spirit inspire a fresh appreciation of myself? Of others? What changes in behavior does this image call forth from me?

3. What do I make of Paul's teaching about baptism as true participation in Christ's death and resurrection? What old ways am I being called to leave behind? How am I being called to "walk in newness of life"?

4. In addition to baptism by water (accompanied by the trinitarian formula), the sacrament involves an anointing with chrism, the sacred oil. How does Paul's reference to anointing help me to value what it means to be "christed"?

5. How often do I reflect on my core identity as a child, a son or daughter, of God? Why is it important for me to do so?

6. In what ways do I reflect to my children (or grandchildren or the children whom I know) the tender, parental love of God? Who has revealed this love to me?

7. What are my deepest fears? How might "fear of the Lord," properly understood, help me to be freed from unhealthy fears?

8. How does Paul's description of the Spirit's assisting us in our prayer console me? How does it inspire me

to fidelity to prayer, especially when it is difficult to persevere?

9. How has God transformed me, through the gift of the Spirit, into the likeness of Christ? In what ways am I being called to witness to hope? To love?

10. Which of the ninefold "fruit of the Spirit" Paul lists in Galatians 5:22-23 do I manifest? In which am I being called to grow?

4

SALVATION

Much more surely then, now that we have been justified by his blood, will we be saved through him from the wrath of God. For if while we were enemies, we were reconciled to God through the death of his Son, much more surely, having been reconciled, will we be saved by his life.

—Romans 5:9–10

Our study of Paul's treatment of the Holy Spirit demonstrated his appreciation for sanctification, the gift of the Spirit that enables his recipients to grow in the ways of holiness. Sanctification is one of several ways in which Paul describes God's saving action through Messiah Jesus. The Letter to the Romans is a fertile source for understanding Pauline soteriology (from the Greek *sōtēria*, "salvation"), a term employed by systematic theologians to describe what salvation through the Christ-event involves. As the citation above illustrates, the apostle maintains that salvation has three "tenses"—past (what God had accomplished through Christ and the gift of the Spirit); present (the current condition of the faithful); and future (the fullness of resurrection life).

The verses preceding 5:9–10 refer to the demonstration of God's love by the death of his Son when human beings were mired in ungodliness and sin (5:6–8), as well as to the outpouring of God's love through the bestowal of the Holy Spirit in human hearts (5:5). Paul then employs a mode of argumentation known by Jews as "light and heavy" (*qal wa-homer*). According to this way of thinking, God has already done the more difficult (that is, the heavier) thing—justifying and reconciling us when we were sinners and enemies. God has thereby revealed his great mercy and magnanimity. Now, how "much more" can God be counted on to do the easier (that is, the lighter) thing, bringing those whom he has saved from spiritual death to resurrected life and glory in the future?

This excerpt includes a number of elements that Paul develops throughout the letter. Before treating them, however, it will be helpful to explain his understanding of the condition of humanity and creation apart from Christ; in other words, from what are people saved? Then we will look at the Apostle's ways of describing salvation under the following headings: redemption, expiation, and forgiveness—all of which pertain to God's dealing with the power of sin and its effects; justification, a term that has evoked much theological controversy; and reconciliation, a theme most relevant in today's context.

FROM WHAT ARE WE SAVED?

It has been remarked that Paul, in coming to appreciate the saving significance of Jesus's death on the cross, then reasoned backward to reflect on what the problem was that the cross addressed. Because Paul was convinced that Christ died for *all* (cf. 2 Cor 5:14), he deduced that the need for salvation was universal. Indeed, he insists that "all have sinned and fall short of the glory of God" (3:23); "all, both Jews and Greeks [Gentiles], are under the power of sin" (3:9). Paul appeals to the Jewish Scriptures to support his gloomy assessment of the human condition apart from Christ. In 3:10–18, he strings together a number of passages that echo the haunting refrain "there is no one": "There is no one who is righteous, not even one; / there is no one who has understanding, / there is no one who seeks God…there is no one who shows kindness, / there is not even one."

The reference to falling short of the glory of God is an allusion to the creation of human beings in the image of God (Gen 1:26–27). Human beings were made to reflect the greatness and grandeur of God; in other words, to give him glory by the way they live. We saw in chapter 2 that Paul regards Adam as both a historical figure and a representative figure, one who stands at the head of those who follow in his disobedience. In 5:12, he famously asserts that "just as sin came into the world through one man [Adam], and death came through sin, and so death spread to all because all have sinned." Adam's primordial disobedience against God's only command to him (cf. Gen 2:17; 3:1–6) led to the coming of the terrible powers of sin (*hamartia*) and death (*thanatos*). According to the Apostle, these two cosmic powers are the great enemies of God's designs for creation.

Notice how Paul personifies sin and death. They enter into the drama of creation like actors on a stage—*Hamartia* enters first, then in its wake arrives *Thanatos*[1] (5:12). Elsewhere in the letter, he says that *Hamartia* enslaves (6:20) those in whom it dwells (7:17), and is a tyrant that holds its victims captive (7:23). The "wages" *Hamartia* pays out is death (both physical and spiritual death; 6:23). The insidious nature of *Hamartia* is such that, as we will see in a moment, it even uses the Jewish Law, a good and holy gift from God, as an opportunity (literally, "a base of operations") from which to arouse harmful passions and desires that lead to death (7:7–12).

While the primordial disobedience brought about this dire situation, Paul holds that since then all human beings have recapitulated

Adam's sin. In his assessment of the guilt of the Gentiles (1:18–32), he explains that their enslavement to sin was the result of their failure to acknowledge God (*asebeia*) and their refusal to give him thanks and praise (1:18, 21), thereby rupturing the divine-human (vertical) relationship. In addition, just as Adam and Eve's sin had deleterious consequences for the relationship between the two of them (cf. Gen 3:16), so rebellion against God has led to the sundering of the bonds of human-human (horizontal) relationships. Paul's vice list in 1:29–31 is a litany of attitudes and actions—such as envy, deceit, gossiping, haughtiness, heartlessness—that break down social relations (cf. Gal 5:19–21; Col 3:5–9). At the head of this list is *adikia*, the lack of righteousness and justice vis-à-vis one's fellow human beings. The Apostle's critique of the human situation before Christ even extends to his own people, the Jews (2:17–24). Though gifted with God's holy Law, they have not been "a light to those who are in darkness" (2:19).[2]

Chief among the vices that plague all who follow in Adam's footsteps is covetousness (*pleonexia*), which Paul elsewhere calls "desire" (*epithymia*; 7:7). This refers to the seemingly insatiable human urge to attain those things and relationships that are thought to bring wealth, power, honor, and satisfaction. It entails seeking "life" in ways other than that offered by God, who is the only one who can bestow true life (cf. 8:5–8). And it is enacted at the expense of others. The mindset of covetousness is as follows: there are limited goods in the world and life is a "zero-sum" game—your gain comes at my expense and vice versa. Consequently, others are regarded as rivals and competitors. Hence the various expressions of antisocial vices in 1:29–31 referred to in the previous paragraph.

The insidious power of *Hamartia* is such that it can use God's good commandment, "You shall not covet" (Exod 20:17; Deut 5:21), as a base of operations to wreak havoc in people's hearts (7:7–8). Here we arrive at an interpretive challenge. In 7:7–25, Paul writes in the first person singular ("I" and "me"). He hauntingly portrays this "I" as indwelled by *Hamartia*, incapable of doing what he knows is the right thing to do. Instead, this "I" does the very thing he knows is wrong (7:15–20). Paul's "I" is utterly perplexed, unable to understand his own actions. The "I," in effect, has become a battleground between warring forces of good and evil within, threatening to tear him apart. His description of the sin-entrapped "I" can sound to modern ears like a person who is helplessly caught up in dysfunction and/or addiction—with the caveat that, for the Apostle, the enslaved "I" is morally responsible for his collusion in the rebellion.

But who is this "I"? A straightforward reading of the text suggests that Paul is speaking autobiographically. But such a reading is untenable. Paul's self-assessment of his life prior to encountering the risen Lord is robustly positive (Gal 1:14; Phil 3:4–6), though he would always regret that his zeal had led him to persecute Christ-believers. Moreover, given what he teaches about the Spirit's empowerment (cf. chapter 3), the description of the "I" in 7:7–25 certainly cannot express his present situation. No, Paul is engaging in the technique called *prosōpopoeïa* (literally, making a person or face [as in a mask]). That is, he is speaking in character; here in character of those who stand in the lineage of the disobedient Adam. The effect is a dramatic portrayal of the human condition apart from the saving grace of God, one that concludes with a desperate cry for help: "Wretched human being [*anthrōpos*] that I am! Who will deliver me?" (7:24; au. trans.).

It is not just the human condition, however, that *Hamartia* adversely affects. In the Genesis story, Adam and Eve's disobedience also harmed the harmonious relationship between them and the earth (cf. "cursed is the ground because of you"; Gen 3:17). Human covetousness and rebellion against God and his ways have had destructive consequences for the earth and the environment, the "home" for all his good creation. As Pope Francis so prophetically challenges in his encyclical *Laudato Si'*, these toxic tendencies prevail today more than ever. Paul hints at this reality in 8:19–22, where he personifies creation as "groaning" and in "bondage to decay." The "futility" that resulted from people's turning away from God and turning selfishly in on themselves (cf. 1:21) is now mirrored in the subjection of creation "to futility, not of its own will" (8:20). In short, the Apostle maintains that both human beings and the very *kosmos* itself stand in dire need of God's saving intervention through Messiah Jesus.

REDEMPTION, EXPIATION, AND FORGIVENESS

We have observed that God's love has been revealed most dramatically in that "while we still were sinners Christ died for us" (5:8). Whereas the disobedience of Adam had death-dealing consequences, the obedience of Jesus, the new Adam, has brought about the possibility of new life (5:15–19). A salutary (the word comes from *salūs*, Latin for "salvation") effect of Jesus's faithfulness-unto-death is that it shattered the bonds of *Hamartia*'s enslaving power, thereby unfettering from its stranglehold all those who receive the gospel proclamation with faith. Paul uses the metaphor of redemption (*apolytrōsis*) to convey this liberating action by God through Messiah Jesus (3:24). Redemption refers to ransoming or buying back hostages or slaves—typically prisoners taken in war. Jesus himself employed this image when he declared that he came "to give his life [as] a ransom (*lytron*) for many" (Mark 10:45).

Redemption is a powerful biblical metaphor. It evokes the exodus event, celebrated by Jews at Passover. The liberation of the Hebrews from their oppression and slavery in Egypt was an expression of compassion and love—not to mention, of mighty power—by God who is faithful to his covenant promises. As God revealed to Moses, "I am the LORD....I have remembered my covenant [with Abraham, Isaac, and Jacob]. Say therefore to the Israelites, 'I am the LORD, and I will free you from the burdens of the Egyptians and deliver you from slavery to them. I will redeem you with an outstretched arm....I will take you as my people, and I will be your God'" (Exod 6:2–7). Paul teaches that God has now performed an even mightier act of liberation from an even stronger oppressive power—that of sin and death. And, as he reminds the Corinthians, God has done so at a great cost: "you were bought with a price" (1 Cor 6:20), the blood of his Son.

While Paul normally uses *hamartia* to refer to "sin" as a personified cosmic force, he employs a different word, *paraptōma*, to convey the notion of "trespass" or "transgression" (e.g., lying and stealing). In this connection, he also understands Jesus's death in cultic and sacrificial terms. In fact, immediately after referring to Jesus's redemptive death, Paul asserts that God "put [Jesus] forward as an expiation, through faithfulness, by means of his blood" (3:25, au. trans.). "Expiation" translates *hilastērion*, the mercy seat that covered the ark of the covenant. On Yom Kippur (the Day of Atonement), the Jewish high priest sprinkled blood from a sacrificed bull and goat over the *hilastērion* in order to perform an act of purification (cf. Lev 16:2–22). The Apostle draws on this atoning imagery in setting forth the significance of Jesus's faithfulness-unto-death, which takes away guilt and brings about "at-*one*-ment," making two parties (God and those whose sins are forgiven) one.

Similarly, Paul asserts that Jesus's death is *peri hamartias* (8:3), a phrase used in the Greek version of Leviticus 9:2 and 14:31 to denote a "sin offering."[3] The sacrificial death of Jesus has brought about the forgiveness of trespasses (4:25). This same imagery lies behind what Paul says in highly condensed fashion in 2 Corinthians 5:21: "For our sake [God] made him to be sin [a sin offering] who knew no sin." That is, Jesus is the unblemished offering of sacrifice. A few verses before the latter passage, Paul makes clear what forgiveness of sins entails: for those who open their hearts to God's mercy, he no longer reckons their trespasses against them (2 Cor 5:19). God has wiped the slate clean, canceling all their debt (cf. Matt 18:27).

At this point, it is helpful to clarify a possible misunderstanding. Note that I have used the word "expiation" rather than "propitiation." On the one hand, *expiation* has the meaning of taking away guilt (the preposition *ex* signifies "out of"), which is accomplished through the atoning death of Jesus. Those who receive the gospel in faith and are baptized are forgiven. On the other hand, *propitiation* connotes an action done to mollify God. This evokes the image of appeasing an angry God to refrain from carrying out his wrath. In chapter 1, we saw how Paul understands the "wrath of God," and that mercy is the prominent divine trait. The sacrificial and cultic imagery used to explicate the significance of Jesus's death is best understood in light of God's loving, saving outreach to restore right relationship with humanity.

In the *Spiritual Exercises*, St. Ignatius of Loyola proposes a beautiful way to pray in light of this mystery of God's merciful love. After contemplating God's goodness and generous love, as well as all the specific blessings he has given to me; and after reflecting honestly about my sinfulness, and the ingratitude and selfishness that lie behind it, I am invited to kneel before a crucifix. There I meditate on how extraordinarily incommensurate is God's loving, merciful outreach to me in my sinfulness, and then consider three questions: What have I done for Christ? What am I doing for Christ? And what ought I do for Christ? Paul offers sound advice, in Colossians 3:13, vis-à-vis the third question: "Bear with one another and, if anyone has a complaint against another, forgive each other; just as the Lord has forgiven you, so you also must forgive." Indeed, those who have received God's merciful compassion through Messiah Jesus should now clothe themselves with "compassion, kindness, humility, meekness, and patience" (Col 3:12).

Redemption, expiation, and forgiveness all convey the notion of freedom. In Galatians 5:1, Paul declares, "For freedom Christ has set us free." With this concise expression, he manages to say a lot about freedom. According to him, freedom has two aspects. The first aspect of freedom is being freed *from* someone or something. As a matter of fact, we have been discussing three ways in which we have been set free: redemption is liberation *from* the enslaving power of *Hamartia*; expiation involves being freed *from* guilt; forgiveness is the release *from* the debt or burden of transgressions. But "freedom from" is only the beginning of what constitutes authentic freedom. The second aspect of freedom—one made possible because of the first—is freedom *for*; recall that it is "for freedom Christ has set us free."

But freed for what? Being freed from the power of *Hamartia* and forgiven our trespasses results (surprise!) in another slavery—this time, being "enslaved to God" (6:22). Paul is most fond of paradoxes. But this "slavery" to God is, in reality, the Spirit-empowered obedience to God's ways as revealed through Christ. Only with the assistance of God's Spirit can we fulfill "the just requirement of the law" (8:4) and be truly free. Paul describes this freedom as our belonging to Jesus so that "we may bear fruit for God" (7:4). This is the freedom to love and serve others after the manner of Jesus, who did not covet or seek to please himself, but rather sought to edify others and to act always for their best interests (15:1–3; Mark 10:45). Paul calls this way of living "walk[ing] in newness of life" (6:4). This understanding of freedom challenges contemporary notions that focus almost exclusively on the demand for personal autonomy, the right for self-determination, and "freedom of choice." Such, however, are but pale intimations of what true freedom means. The wretched "I" of 7:7–25 has been set free and energized by the Spirit for love and service.

One final point: Although Paul's soteriological concern is primarily anthropological, he also recognizes that God's work of redemption involves *all* of creation—"creation itself will be set free from its bondage to decay" (8:21). While the full renewal and restoration of the *kosmos* await God's definitive future action, the gift of freedom for the present entails our becoming the good stewards of creation God intended us to be (Gen 1:26–28). Pope Francis has acknowledged that the Genesis text—"let them have dominion over"—has too often been misinterpreted to condone the greedy exploitation of the earth's resources. The pontiff's call for concrete actions—enacted with gratitude to God, and with concern for future generations—to sustain ecosystems, to preserve the environment, and to restore the life-giving impetus of mother earth is an important extension and appropriation of the Apostle's thought.

JUSTIFICATION BY FAITH

Paul's most famous contribution to soteriology is what he says about justification—or more precisely, the justification by faith. In 3:30, he writes, "God is one; and he will justify the circumcised on the ground of faith and the uncircumcised through that same faith." The first question to ask is by *whose* faith (*pistis*) are people justified? While many translations add the possessive pronoun "their" before faith (referring to the human response of faith by both Jews and Gentiles), the pronoun is not in the Greek text. The NRSV appropriately omits the pronoun, thereby maintaining Paul's careful articulation.

The *pistis* through which God justifies is, in the first place, the faithfulness of Messiah Jesus, his faithfulness/obedience-unto-death on the cross (as we saw in chapter 2). Christ's faithfulness is the revelation par excellence of God's righteousness (*dikaiosynē*), his covenant faithfulness. Justification (*dikaiōsis* and *dikaiōma*—from the same root as *dikaiosynē*) by faith, according to Paul, has its roots in the fact that God is faithful (cf. 3:3)—faithful to his covenant promises, indeed, faithful to his very character. Recall that God's righteousness means not only that he is just; he is also merciful in making right what has gone wrong through human rebellion and sinfulness. In addition, God's righteousness points to his sense of fairness. As Paul indicates in 2:11, "God shows no partiality." This quality is manifested in the fact that God has reached out to all, Jews and Gentiles, through Messiah Jesus (3:30).

In 3:21–22, Paul declares that God's righteousness has been revealed through Messiah Jesus's faithfulness-unto-death "for all who believe" or, as I prefer to translate (for reasons that will become clear), "for all who have faith." The covenant faithfulness of God, mediated through Jesus's faithfulness, in turn calls for a human response. God's gift of redemption and forgiveness is to be received through faith, in imitation of Abraham's response to God's call and promises to him of countless progeny and a homeland (4:3; cf. Gen 15:6). Trusting belief in God's offer of new life is the proper response to the good news. This human response, made possible by God's grace, is what is often more narrowly understood as the faith that justifies. But as we have just observed, Paul's teaching of "justification by faith" is much richer.

God justifies (*dikaioō*) those who thus open themselves to his gift: "they are now justified by his grace as a gift" (3:24). The verb *dikaioō*, in its most fundamental sense, has a forensic meaning. In his merciful justice, God as judge declares "justified" or "in the right" all those who respond with trusting faith in the gospel proclamation and are baptized as an expression of that faith (in the case of infants, the faith is professed by parents and godparents). This declaration of "justified" (being in right relationship with God) is a wholly unmerited grace, as Paul makes perfectly clear when he writes that Christ died for us "while we still were sinners," mired in the condition of being "ungodly" and even "enemies" of God (5:6–10). No human works or merits come into play at this point. Justification is a manifestation of God's "grace" and "free gift"

(5:15–17). The *Catechism*'s comment that the justification of sinners "is the *most excellent work of God's love*" (CCC 1994; italics in the original) is most apropos.

What seems to complicate things is Paul's statement in 2:13 that "it is not the hearers of the law who are righteous (*dikaioi*) in God's sight, but the *doers* of the law who will be justified (*dikaiothēsontai*)" (au. emphasis). In this passage, he suggests that God's justification is based on deeds, that is, on works pertaining to the Jewish Law. But how does this jibe with Paul's remark in 3:20 that no one will be justified in God's sight "by deeds prescribed by the law"? Or with what he says in Galatians 2:16: "A person is justified not by the works of the law but through faith"? It seems that Paul is inconsistent, even contradictory. And in fact, some commentators dismiss the statement in 2:13 about *doing* the Law as not representative of his thinking on justification. But I operate under the presumption that the Apostle's teaching is coherent throughout.

To make sense of all this, it is crucial to appreciate that Paul also speaks of justification as a future act, one that will take place at the final judgment (14:10). Notice the future tense verb "will be justified" in 2:13 (the passive voice indicates that *God* is the one who will justify). At the final judgment, God/Christ[4] will judge people on the basis of their deeds (2 Cor 5:10; cf. Matt 25:31–46). But it is necessary to understand that, for Paul, these deeds are Spirit-enabled acts of love that are the fulfillment of what the Jewish Law intended all along (8:4). Walking in the way of Jesus's self-giving love—only made possible because of God's gift of the Spirit—is what fulfills the Law (13:8–10). At the last judgment, the divine verdict for those who have thus been "doers" of the Law will be "justified," one that will confirm God's initial declaration, by grace, of "in the right" when they first accepted the good news of salvation.

We can now clarify three further points about justification by faith according to Paul. The first involves what he means by "faith" (*pistis*). At a base level, faith refers to the response of trusting belief in "the gospel of God" (1:1). But Paul also teaches that "the only thing that counts is faith working through love" (Gal 5:6). Faith is ultimately and most integrally expressed by an *entire* way of life. Strikingly, Paul says that faith "works" (*energeō*, from which is "energy")—that is, is expressed—through love. It is this Spirit-empowered way of life, manifested in deeds, that leads to the final verdict of "in the right." For this reason, the verb *dikaioō* can also connote "make righteous." God, through the gift of the Spirit, empowers self-giving deeds of love that are the ultimate expression of righteousness (cf. 2 Cor 5:21). As the *Catechism* remarks, justification also involves the sanctification of one's whole being (CCC 1995, citing 6:19). Catholic tradition supplements the forensic interpretation of justification with a transformative one.

The second point regards the declaration in Galatians 2:16 that no one is justified "by the works of the law" (cf. Rom 3:20). There, Paul employs a technical phrase, *ex ergōn nomou*, to signify practices (especially circumcision, dietary laws, and Sabbath observance) that marked off Jews from other people. In the context of Galatians, where he wrote to communities *made up exclusively of Gentiles*, the Apostle insists that the latter do not have to become Jews in order to enter the people God is forming around Christ. (That this was a critical issue in the early Church is witnessed to by the lengthy treatment of it in Acts 10–15.) The Gentiles' baptism is sufficient for that. Rather than such "works of the law," it is first and foremost the faithfulness of Messiah Jesus[5] that justifies them, bringing them into covenant relationship with God.

This leads to a third point. While our focus has been on the justification of individual believers, Paul's emphasis is in fact communal. The impetus of God's covenant faithfulness is to call and form a *people* whose distinguishing characteristic is *pistis*—believing trust in God's goodness and promises that have been fulfilled in Christ, and faithfulness in embodying God's holiness to others (Lev 19:2). This "people" is the family of faith that God promised to Abraham, a family comprised of both Gentile and Jewish believers (4:9–17). God's act of justification thus also entails his declaration that those who respond with believing trust in the gospel now have the status of membership in this family of faith.

RECONCILIATION

We began this chapter by quoting Paul's "light and heavy" (*qal wa-homer*) argument in 5:9–10. This remarkable statement contains much. For our purposes, two comments suffice. First, these verses are a good example of how, for Paul, salvation is both a present experience—we have been justified; we have been reconciled—and a future reality—we shall be saved. In terms of the latter, he refers to the fullness of resurrection life, when the Lord Jesus Christ "will transform our humble bodies that they may be conformed to the body of his glory" (Phil 3:21; NRSV alt. trans.). This is when the last enemy, death (*Thanatos*), will be destroyed, and God will be "all in all" (1 Cor 15:28). Second, Paul describes justification and reconciliation in a parallel manner, thereby suggesting a close connection between them. While reconciliation language is not as prominent in his writings as that of justification, it is no exaggeration to claim that reconciliation lies at the center of his theology and spirituality.

The theme of reconciliation presumes a prior situation of enmity. The enmity at issue for Paul is that resulting from human rebellion against God and his ways. Disobedience and sin ruptured the divine-human relationship. It also led to alienation among peoples and to damaged relationships with creation. The remarkable feature of God's reconciling work through Christ is that God—the "wronged" party, as it were—is the one who, in his magnanimous love, acted unilaterally to restore the various broken relationships.

In fact, *only* God could do so. He is therefore the "God of peace" (16:20) who has established the possibility of peace with him (5:1). It is little wonder that Paul rejoices in announcing God's magnanimity and love: "We *celebrate* God through our Lord Jesus Christ, through whom we have now received our reconciliation" (5:11; au. trans.). Such joy is a gift of the Spirit, as is peace (Gal 5:22).

God's work of reconciliation has also created the possibility of being at peace with others, including those who were formerly hostile. Paul employs dramatic imagery in Ephesians 2:14 to express the reconciliation between Jews and Gentiles that God has brought about through Messiah Jesus: "[Christ] is our peace; in his flesh he has made both groups into one and has broken down the dividing wall, that is, the hostility between us." Many scholars argue that the "dividing wall" alludes to the wall in the Jerusalem temple complex that separated the court of the Gentiles from the inner courts. It was thus a symbol of division. But through the cross, this division has been overcome so that Christ "might reconcile both groups to God in one body" (Eph 2:16). In our time, the tearing down of the Berlin Wall in 1989 was the catalyst for uniting East and West Germany. Conversely, the call from some to erect a wall along the southern United States' border is a manifestation of the divisions Christ came to overthrow—if his followers (and others) choose to live out the gift of reconciliation and seek ways that make for true and lasting peace.[6]

Indeed, according to Paul, God's work of reconciling the world to himself is more than a gift; it is also a task or mission for those who have received reconciliation. God has given to the Church the message and ministry of reconciliation (2 Cor 5:18–19). Fundamentally, the mission of proclaiming the gospel includes calling people to be reconciled to God (2 Cor 5:20). Authentic reconciliation with God, however, must also be enacted through reconciliation between peoples. One of Paul's more famous statements is Galatians 3:28—"There is no longer Jew or Greek, there is no longer slave or free, there is no longer male and female; for all of you are one in Christ Jesus." The Apostle was passionate about forming communities that do not allow ethnic, cultural, socioeconomic, and gender differences—real as they are—to prevent members from regarding and treating one another, first and foremost, as fellow family members in Christ.

Communities that embody unity-in-diversity bear eloquent witness to the reconciling power of God. One of my great joys as a priest is to assist in a parish that is rich in diversity—especially in its ethnic makeup. Once in a while, during the homily, I invite people to look around the sanctuary to appreciate how diverse we are. I ask, "Where else does such a variety of people come together as one?" Of course, gathering to worship is not enough; the community is to live out this unity in its day-to-day existence. Paul teaches that doing so has revelatory value. When he states, as in Ephesians 3:10, "that through the church the wisdom of God in its rich variety might now be made known to the rulers and authorities in the heavenly places," he is talking about the Church's witness to a different way of being. Its expression of unity-in-diversity, committed to peace—rather than to rivalry, competition, and enmity—is testimony to the countercultural possibilities of God's reconciling love.

One particular expression of reconciled unity-in-diversity is the sharing of resources. A recurring topic in Paul's letters is the collection he took up from his (mostly) Gentile churches for the church in Jerusalem (Gal 2:10; I Cor 16:1–4; 2 Cor 8:1—9:15; Rom 15:25–31). While the original impetus for the collection was to address the financial need of the Jerusalem believers, it took on much greater significance for him. Paul saw it as a symbol of the reconciliation between Jews and Gentiles effected by Jesus's cross and resurrection. Because the Gentiles had received spiritual benefits from Jerusalem, it was fitting that they share material resources with the church there (15:27). This would be a concrete manifestation of the *koinōnia*, the "communion" and "fellowship," of the

Church. Today, it is edifying to see many parishes engaged in such mutual cooperation across distance and cultures, especially when human resources are added to financial ones.

To be sure, for the Church to proclaim God's work of reconciliation with integrity, her members must continually strive toward mutual forgiveness. Paul models this in 2 Corinthians. An incident occurred between him and a community member that caused misunderstanding, hurt, and division. Work on the collection came to a standstill, and the community seemed to be of different minds vis-à-vis their founding Apostle. After receiving a letter from Paul (now lost to us) that helped them to realize the grief caused to him by the incident, many in the church in Corinth punished the offending member, probably by ostracizing him (cf. 2 Cor 2:1–6; 7:8–12). Part of the Apostle's motivation in writing 2 Corinthians is to be reconciled with the community as a whole (6:11–13; 7:2–4). And one way he encourages reconciliation is to exhort the church to receive back in love the offending member, because he himself has already forgiven that person (2:7–11). The work of reconciliation, like charity, begins at home.

Paul's soteriology is powerful and inspiring. His dark portrait of human disobedience, rebellion, and sin—and their effects—provides the contrast that makes the brilliant light of God's saving grace shine all the more brightly. In the redemption brought about through Messiah Jesus, God has acted to break the enslaving bonds of the two great enemies, (personified) sin and death. Christ's expiating death on the cross is atonement for our sins. God's gifts of forgiveness and justification, of being declared "in the right," bring with them the freedom to love and serve God and others. The gift of reconciliation carries with it the task to be agents of peace who strive for unity-in-diversity. It is Paul's teaching about the reconciled and peace-seeking community of faith—that is, the Church—that we treat next.

QUESTIONS FOR PRAYER AND REFLECTION

1. What do I make of Paul's depiction of personified sin (*Hamartia*) and death (*Thanatos*)? What do I make of his emphasis, in the vice lists, on attitudes and actions that break apart relationships and community?

2. How does Paul's portrayal of the enslaved "I" in 7:7–25 strike me?

3. How have I known the power of God's redemption? In what ways have I experienced being freed by God from something, someone, or a situation that was holding me back?

4. How am I inspired by Paul's understanding of Jesus's death on the cross as sacrificial? How does this understanding challenge me? Why is it important to recognize the divine love that is manifested on the cross?

5. What do I first think about when I hear the word "freedom"? In what ways does Paul's teaching about "freedom from" and—especially—"freedom for" invite me to expand my appreciation and exercise of freedom?

6. How has reading this chapter helped me understand "justification by faith"? What difference does starting with God's covenant fidelity, as revealed through Christ's faithfulness-unto-death, make in grasping what Paul says?

7. How does Paul's insistence that "the only thing that counts is faith working through love" (Gal 5:6) impact what I think is meant by the life of faith?

8. What does God's taking the initiative to bring about the possibility of reconciliation with him and others contribute to my appreciation of who God is and how he acts?

9. How have I experienced reconciliation with God? With others? With creation? With whom do I feel the need and desire to be reconciled? How am I being called to be an agent of peace and reconciliation?

10. How have I experienced unity-in-diversity in my parish or faith community? In what practical ways can I contribute to it?

5

CHURCH

For as in one body we have many members, and not all the members have the same function, so we, who are many, are one body in Christ, and individually we are members one of another.

—Romans 12:4–5

We conclude our treatment of the Letter to the Romans by examining what Paul has to say in it about the Church. This area of theology is known as ecclesiology (the term comes from *ekklēsia*, the word rendered "church," though it can refer more broadly to "assembly"—for example, a legislative body or a more informal gathering of people). To focus on Paul's ecclesiology is fitting because much of his time and energies were expended on establishing and nurturing *communities* of believers. While he is rightly regarded as a great theologian, it is important to appreciate that he was first and foremost a missionary and pastor. Moreover, Paul lived in a time—unlike our own (at least in the West)—when people thought primarily in terms of group identity rather than individual identity. In other words, one's identity was understood and expressed most fundamentally in terms of belonging to a particular group.

The passage cited above appears near the beginning of a section in which Paul offers an extended exhortation to the believers in Rome (12:1—15:13). Following his lengthy exposition of the gospel (1:16—11:36), he now sets forth the implications of the good news for their daily lives (cf. the "therefore" in 12:1). Strikingly, Paul grounds his exhortations in "the mercies of God." In light of God's merciful outreach to sinful humanity through the sending of his Son and the gift of the Spirit, what is the appropriate response? Paul begins by encouraging the Roman faithful to present themselves "as a living sacrifice, holy and acceptable to God." They are to comport themselves in such a way—day in and day out—that gives glory and praise to God. And, as Paul makes clear in 12:4–5, they are to do so in the context of living as members of the Body of Christ. The Church is the "arena" in which Christian spirituality is enacted.

Although Paul was not the founder of the Christ movement in Rome, his letter to the believers there reveals his typical concerns as found throughout his writings: that the community of faith appropriate and mature in their identity as "one body in Christ"; that they learn how to welcome and build up one another in love, especially in potentially divisive situations; and that they bear authentic witness to outsiders to the life-giving power of the gospel. But first, it will be helpful to give some background information about the makeup and circumstances of the Roman faithful.

THE CHURCH(ES) IN ROME

What do we know about the believers in Rome and their situation when Paul wrote to them? Near the end of the letter, he sends greetings to various members—including two dozen by name—of at least five house churches in the city (16:3–16). Given that Paul had not yet been to Rome, it is remarkable that he knew so many of the faithful there. This datum speaks to the high mobility of the early Church.

An example of this mobility is the couple Prisca and Aquila, the first two names on the list. Paul first met them when he came to Corinth. According to Acts 18:2–3, the couple had been part of a group of Jews—both Jewish believers in Christ and Jews who did not so believe—who had been exiled from Rome by the emperor Claudius (in 49 CE).[1] Paul stayed with Prisca and Aquila, and worked together with them as tentmakers. After his eighteen-month ministry in Corinth, the couple moved to Ephesus to lay the foundations for his ministry there (cf. Acts 18:18—19:1). When the exiles were allowed to return to Rome at the beginning of the reign of Nero (in 54 CE), Prisca and Aquila went back. As was the case in Ephesus (cf. I Cor 16:8, 19), they hosted a (local) church in their home. Paul pays this couple lofty tribute: They "work with me in Christ Jesus, and [they] risked their necks for my life, to whom not only I give thanks, but also all the churches of the Gentiles" (16:3–4). Prisca and Aquila were at the core of his apostolic team that had a special ministry to proclaim the good news to Gentiles.

A notable feature of the list of people whom Paul greets is the number of women who appear on it, most of whom are labeled in one manner or other as serving the Lord. One of the women is Junia who, along with Andronicus (likely her husband), is described as "prominent among the apostles" (16:7). In Paul's understanding, an apostle is one who has seen the risen Lord Jesus and been given a particular mission. Moreover, just before the list of greetings, he commends to the Roman believers Phoebe, who is "a deacon of the church at Cenchreae" (a seaport of Corinth) and a "benefactor." Paul sends her ahead of him to prepare for his stay and ministry in Rome. It is very likely that she was the bearer of the Letter to the Romans, and that she was the first person to have proclaimed and explained it. The fact that Paul has a number of women helping in his mission belies the stereotype of him as a misogynist.[2] Actions speak louder than words, and his practice of having women as part of his missionary team is a salutary invitation for the Church today to consider ways to call forth and empower them.

As mentioned above, Paul alludes to the presence of house churches (cf. 16:5—"the church in [Prisca and Aquila's] house"). The early Church met in homes of wealthier members. Membership in these house churches certainly involved geographical proximity. Other factors were also involved, such as trades/professions and ethnicity. Scholars are in general agreement that synagogues were the source from which the gospel was initially proclaimed in Rome. By the time the Apostle wrote to the believers there (ca. 56–57 CE), however, the majority of the community were Gentiles, not Jews.

Some of the tensions that lay behind Paul's exhortations stem from Jewish religious practices. He comments on quarrels over food and observance of days (14:1–6). These refer to disputes over the propriety of eating meats not properly butchered and/or involved in pagan sacrifice, as well as disputes over whether to observe certain Jewish feast days and the Sabbath. While it is natural to think that the community was split entirely along Jewish and Gentile lines, it would be overly simplistic. Paul is an example of a Jew who was "free" concerning practices he formerly held to be essential (cf. 14:14), and many Gentile converts were attracted to the ways of Judaism. For our purposes, it is crucial to appreciate just how important these issues were (and analogously still are today). It matters a great deal whether believers agree or not about how they gather for table fellowship and how they worship together.

The expulsion of leading Jews (including Christ-believers) and their subsequent return also caused some challenges and difficulties among the Roman house churches. A little historical imagination can help us here. The expulsion would have left a leadership vacuum—at least in some of the house churches. Things can change quickly over a short period of time (and the exile lasted about five years). Gentile members likely gained some ascendency. But then what happens when the exiles return to a new situation and context? How do the various house churches interact? It is easy to imagine a number of potential sources of conflict.

This background illuminates many features in Romans, two of which we take up here. One is Paul's emphasis that the Church—including the house churches founded in Rome—is the fulfillment of the promises made to Abraham that he would be the father of many descendants, *both* Gentiles and Jews, whose distinguishing characteristic is faith (4:11–12, 16). He wants the faithful in Rome to recognize that God's plan all along has been to bring Jews and Gentiles into a single family of faith. They are thus to live as a reconciled and united community conformed to the image of Jesus, "the firstborn within a large family" (8:29). As we saw in the previous chapter, such unity-in-diversity bears witness to God's reconciling love.

A second feature is Paul's use of the allegory of a cultivated olive tree to remind the Gentiles of their place in the divine plan (11:17–24). In the background, here, is that some of the Gentile believers may have interpreted the success of the Gentile mission (especially seen in light of the fact that most Jews were not responding with faith to the gospel message) and the expulsion of Jews from Rome as signs that God had rejected Israel. Paul insists that is not the case. Gentile believers are, as it were, wild olive branches God has grafted onto his tree, a metaphor for God's people. The natural branches are Jewish believers (like the Apostle). The branches that have been broken off denote unbelieving Jews. But Paul does not want the Gentile believers to boast about their new status or to gloat over the broken branches. If God is able to graft wild (that is, unnatural) branches onto the tree, then he can surely regraft the broken (but natural) branches onto it.

Both Paul's teaching about the Church as the Gentile-and-Jew family of faith and the olive tree allegory require careful interpretation today, especially for Christian-Jewish relations. It is crucially important to stress that Paul is not supersessionist; he does not say that the Church replaces Israel or that the Jews have been rejected. Indeed, he asserts that God's call and gifts to the Jewish people are irrevocable (11:29). And, although Paul does not offer an explanation as to when and how, he is convinced that "all Israel will be saved" (11:26). Two thousand years later, in a totally different context, where there is no overlap of membership between the Church and Israel (as there was for Paul), Jews and Christians can love, respect, and learn from one another as they both await the Messiah—in the case of Jews, his coming; in the case of Christians, his *return* in glory. In the meantime, Christians can and should appreciate their Jewish roots.

"ONE BODY IN CHRIST"

The Gentile and Jewish makeup of the house churches in Rome gives some flavor to Paul's teaching that the *ekklēsia* is "one body in Christ" (12:5), the image cited at the beginning of this chapter. The life of faith takes place in the context of a community consisting of diverse members. Indeed, the image of "body" evokes several connotations. First, it is an organic image, instructing that the Church is a *living* entity. While beautiful buildings inspire awe and facilitate worship, it is essential to remember that the Church refers primarily to the people who comprise it. Second, "body" emphasizes the interdependence of its members, who are "all in it together." Each and every member is essential. And an important implication, as Paul says elsewhere, is—or at least should be—that "if one member suffers, all suffer together with it; if one member is honored, all rejoice together with it" (I Cor 12:26).

Third, "body" signals that the members have a common purpose, as suggested by the addition of the phrase "in Christ" to "one body." This addition indicates not only that the risen Lord is the source of the Church's life, but also that he enables communities of faith to mediate his presence in space and time, a point to which we will return shortly. Although Paul does not identify the community as the Body *of* Christ as he does in I Corinthians 12:27—"you are the body of Christ and individually members of it"—his meaning in Romans 12:5 rests on that identification. What he leaves implicit is the empowerment of the Holy Spirit, who bestows the various "gifts" (*charismata*) upon members so that they can build up the body, strive for unity, and serve the common good.

Paul's writings contain different, albeit complementary, lists of such Spirit-bestowed gifts. In I Corinthians 12:28, he sets forth a number of special gifts, such as inspired teachings, the ability to heal, and speaking in tongues. In Ephesians 4:11, he lists a number of what we might call offices or officially designated positions, such as apostles, prophets, evangelists, pastors, and teachers. In Romans 12:6–8, the focus is on specific *ministries* and on how they should be enacted. The list Paul provides for the Roman believers is a good reminder that at the core of the Church's identity is its call to ministry. This list gives many ways of how they are empowered, as *ekklēsia*, to flourish. Moreover, it can serve as a litmus test for present-day communities to see whether they are being faithful to their identity and call.

Significantly, Paul gives pride of place to prophecy (12:6). People today tend to reduce the meaning of prophecy to the prediction of the future. That is not what Paul means. Rather, prophecy refers, in the first place, to the gift to recognize God's presence in the community. It involves the discernment of God's will, which leads to the communication of his life-giving Word for current circumstances and situations. Thus, at the heart of the life of the *ekklēsia* is its attentiveness and responsiveness to the Word of God.

Prayerful listening precedes proclamation. "Service" (au. trans. of *diakonia*), the second item on Paul's list (12:7), is to be the distinguishing characteristic of *all* ministries, especially for those in authority and leadership (as implied in the sixth item: "the leader, in diligence"). This is in line with Jesus's own life and ministry (Mark 10:45—"The Son of Man came not to be served but to serve").

The remaining items, while at first glance appearing rather ordinary, also contain much food for thought. Teaching allows for maturation in the life of faith. It is no accident that the word for "disciple," *mathētēs*, means "learner." The life of faith is a lifelong process of learning and appropriating the ways of God as revealed through Christ. Exhortation points to the ways by which members are encouraged to fidelity. Encouragement (another way to translate *paraklēsis*) thus should also be a mark of the Church's ministry. Generosity is to undergird the provision of spiritual and material assistance to needy members of the *ekklēsia*. And not just to insiders, but also to all those whose plight calls for a compassionate response, as indicated in the last (but not least) item on the list: the Church as Christ's Body should practice acts of mercy, as Pope Francis reminded us by calling for the Holy Year of Mercy in 2016.

Paul follows the description of the *charismata* with a series of exhortations to enact in concrete ways what it means to be "one body in Christ" (12:9–13, 15–16). His concern here is with the community's growth. Members of the Church should always act out of "genuine" love, the *agapē* that is committed to acting for the benefit of others. To love in this manner is to "be bubbling over in the Spirit" (12:11, au. trans.). Paul also stresses the extension of hospitality, something most relevant in the context of the network of house churches in Rome. The door of each house church should be open to any and all members, thereby inculcating the unity-in-diversity the Church is called to manifest. Sensitivity to others and their difficulties leads the faithful to compassionate outreach. To this end, the Apostle encourages the community to avoid arrogance and to "associate with the lowly" (12:16) among them.

Paul's call for "hospitality to strangers" (12:13) and association with the "lowly" (*tapeinoi*) merits more attention, especially in today's context. Warfare, unspeakable violence, famine, and/or lack of economic opportunity have led millions of people to migrate from their homelands and to seek refuge elsewhere. To be sure, the situation is complex and multifaceted. But much of the rhetoric today about national security is grounded in fearmongering, with an alarming lack of empathy for the tragic plight of fellow human beings. Paul's teaching about hospitality and association with the lowly can be a clarion call for Christians to engage in their civic duties, advocating for those who are looking for a safe place to live, to raise their families, and to have dignified work. He elsewhere refers to God as the one "who encourages/comforts the lowly" (2 Cor 7:6, au. trans.). Those "called forth" by God to be members of the *ekklēsia* (the literal sense of the term) are to have the same concern and commitment.

This latter point is an illustration of what Paul means by referring to local assemblies as "the body of Christ." At one level, the image functions as a metaphor, comparable to the notion of the "body politic." But at a deeper level, Paul intends more than a metaphor. Local assemblies of Christ-followers are, in fact, to mediate his presence in the here and now. While individuals can, as they progress in the life of the Spirit, become "images" of God after the manner of Jesus, the image of God par excellence, it is as the community of faith—in which the whole far exceeds the sum of its parts—that they most effectively incarnate Christ. And the community does so by continuing the ministry in which Jesus engaged as he inaugurated the kingdom of God. Central to that ministry was Jesus's love and care for the lowly, the *tapeinoi*, who elicited his compassion (cf., e.g., Matt 11:28–30).

Although Paul employs the image of the Body of Christ in Romans with reference to the local community, his description of the collection for the church in Jerusalem (15:26–27) shows that he also understands the larger Church to be a single body. As we saw in the last chapter, he regarded the collection as an expression of the reconciliation God has brought about between Gentiles and Jews. While this reconciliation is realized in local communities of believers, the Body of Christ as the Gentile and Jew family of faith transcends local instances. In Colossians and Ephesians in particular, the Apostle refers to the Church as "body" on a more global, even cosmic scale, with Christ as its head (Col 1:18—"[Christ] is the head of the body, the church"). Hence the claims for the oneness and catholicity of the Church in the Nicene Creed: "I believe in one, holy, catholic, and apostolic Church."

ACTING IN LOVE IN POTENTIALLY DIVISIVE SITUATIONS

The Letter to the Romans provides a window into Paul's pastoral response to potentially divisive issues among members of the house churches in Rome. One issue, as pointed out above, involved food. Some members of the community—the so-called strong in faith—insisted that all foods could be eaten (14:2) since "nothing is unclean in itself" (14:14). Other members ate only vegetables to avoid meat tainted by pagan sacrifice and/or not properly drained of blood (that is, not kosher). Another issue was whether or not to observe Jewish festival days and/or the Sabbath. Since table fellowship and occasions for worship were involved, the stakes were high—whether the disputes were within a particular house church or between house churches. Although these specific controversies might not seem relevant for Christians today, the Apostle's way of approaching them provides helpful guidelines for present-day discernment in the Church.

Paul responds to the controversies over food and worship in two steps. In the first step (14:1–12), he exhorts all the faithful in Rome to self-examination because he detects two highly problematic attitudes. On the one hand, the "strong" tend to look condescendingly on and despise those members they regard as "weak"[3] in working out the implications of the life of faith. On the other hand, the latter tend to judge and condemn the "strong" as acting immorally. At this point, Paul does not take sides. Rather, he reminds the community that God has already welcomed each and every member in his merciful love. Those whom God has so welcomed are now to welcome one another and grow in mutual respect and tolerance. Moreover, Paul calls on members of both sides of the debates to reflect on *why* they practice what they do. All is to be done to give glory and thanks to God. The first order of business, then, is to be self-reflective and not critical of others.

Paul puts his finger here on a chronic problem. The dynamics described in 14:1–12 are eerily similar to those that often play out today in the Church among so-called progressives and traditionalists. One side condescends; the other judges. Similar dynamics are at work in the political arena between red-state voters and blue-state voters. Both in society and in the Church, polemics only lead to polarization. The "body"—the body politic and the "one body in Christ"—is rendered asunder. To be clear, Paul's response is not a concession to relativism, to "I'm okay, you're okay" and "Can't we all just get along?" But it is important to acknowledge that there are things that people of good will can disagree about. His exhortations to the Roman house churches are helpful for inculcating mutual respect and critical self-examination.

But Paul then goes a step further in 14:13—15:6. He challenges the "strong" to look at the situation with different lenses. Rather than insist on their being right in their opinion, they are to be sensitive to those members of the community whose consciences do not yet allow them to partake of meat. The "strong" are warned "never to put a stumbling block or hindrance in the way of another" (14:13; the NRSV's translation aptly captures the sense of *skandalon*). Instead of looking down on others as "weak," they are to regard them as brothers and sisters—and not only as brothers and sisters, but as brothers and sisters *for whom Christ died* (14:15). If Jesus could lay down his life for us when we were still sinners and enemies (cf. 5:8, 10), then surely we can make much smaller sacrifices out of love and consideration for one another.

Paul offers a similar challenge to the church in Corinth, where there was division regarding the propriety of eating food that was associated with pagan sacrifice (I Cor 8:1–13).[4] In exhorting the "strong" in Corinth, Paul holds himself up as an example. While he has "rights" as an apostle—such as to marry and to receive payment for proclaiming the gospel (I Cor 9:4–5)—he does not insist on exercising them. He even sets aside his "rights." Paul has chosen celibacy in order to have greater freedom to pursue single-mindedly "the affairs of the Lord" (I Cor 7:32–35); and he preaches the gospel free of charge in order to communicate the graced quality of its message (I Cor 9:15–18). It is this setting aside of one's "rights" in freedom and love in order to serve others that he has in mind when he later exhorts the Corinthians to "be imitators of me, as I am of Christ" (I Cor 11:1).

Returning to Romans, Paul similarly exhorts the "strong" to imitate Jesus: "Each of us must please our neighbor for the good purpose of building up the neighbor. For Christ did not please himself" (15:2–3). This is how the community of faith is built up in love. Such loving regard for others, accepting and taking them where they are, will help all the members to mature in living out more fully the implications of their faith commitment—and to promote "harmony with one another, in accordance with Christ Jesus" (15:5). Interestingly, this section contains one of the few references Paul makes to the kingdom of God: "The kingdom of God is not food and drink but righteousness and peace and joy in the Holy Spirit" (14:17). That is, members of the *ekklēsia* should stay grounded in God's righteousness as revealed through Christ's death—which has brought reconciliation and peace—and through the outpouring of the Spirit. Once again, the Apostle intimates the theme of God's mercy.

Harmony in the community of faith enables the Church "with one voice [to] glorify the God and Father of our Lord Jesus Christ" (15:6). It is surely no accident that Paul concludes his exhortations to the house churches in Rome with rich liturgical imagery (15:7–13). The mutual welcoming of Gentile and Jewish believers in the community of faith is an eloquent expression of the reconciliation God has brought about through Christ. The flip side is that the appropriate response to this manifestation of God's love is to come together to sing his praises. Paul thereby suggests that the Church is most "Church" when it gathers as one—"no longer Jew or Greek,...no longer slave or free,...no longer male and female; for all of you are one in Christ Jesus" (Gal 3:28)—in the liturgical assembly to praise and glorify God.

At the heart of the liturgical celebration is the Eucharist. Yet there is no mention of the Eucharist in Romans. In fact, the only reference to the "Lord's supper" in Paul's writings is in I Corinthians 11:17–34. And in this case, he only brings up the topic because he has heard of abuses at the celebration![5] This exception, however, reveals that the Eucharist was celebrated in the Pauline communities. Ironically, its centrality can account for the relative silence about it. Paul simply *presumes* its celebration. Moreover, his indignation at the behavior of some of the Corinthians shows just how important the Eucharist was for the Apostle.

Paul's critique of the celebration of the "Lord's supper" calls for further comment. He declares that "all who eat and drink without discerning the body, eat and drink judgment against themselves" (I Cor 11:29). What Paul means here by "discerning the body" is not whether one believes in the Real Presence; rather, his concern is that members of the community recognize the presence of Christ in *all* their fellow members and conducts themselves accordingly. In other words, do they (and do we) show reverence to the Body of Christ that is the Church, as present in the local assembly? Pope Francis reminds us of the social character of the Eucharist. Reverent reception of the body and blood of Christ entails reaching out in love to others, particularly the suffering and poor around us.

RELATIONS WITH OUTSIDERS

The Church does not exist solely for the sake of its members, nor is it to withdraw from the world around it. Paul makes this clear in I Corinthians 5:9–10: "I wrote to you in my letter [now lost to us] not to associate with sexually immoral persons—not at all meaning the immoral of this world, or the greedy and robbers, or idolaters, since you would then need to go out of the world." The Church exists in the world. To be sure, much of what Paul writes concerns *intra*-community issues. The churches he founded were small in size and were in many ways vulnerable vis-à-vis dangerous outside influences. Paul had to be concerned with their survival and—especially in the case of Gentile converts—with how they adjusted to a new way of being (cf., e.g., I Cor 6:9–11). Nevertheless, he was also aware of the witness value of the Church. Indeed, we just noted the importance of worship. The Apostle insists on harmonious and ordered ways of being together in the assembly. One reason is that outsiders might observe the community at prayer and "bow down before God and worship him, declaring, 'God is really among you'" (I Cor 14:25).

In addition to worship, Paul is sanguine about the witness value of local communities that embody the ways of Messiah Jesus. While the witness of individuals is inspiring, the collective witness of the *ekklēsia* as the Body of Christ is even more effective. In fact, the most persuasive witness to the power of the gospel is the transformation of peoples of different ethnic, cultural, and socioeconomic backgrounds so that they now regard and treat one another as family—as brothers and sisters in Christ. The coming together of Gentiles and Jews, of slaves and free, of rich and poor, into the single family of faith bears witness to the world that God's saving action through Christ actually does make a difference in the here and now.

The unity-in-diversity of the Body of Christ, lived in mutual love and service, also stands as a prophetic *counter*example against prevailing cultural values (recall the reference in the last chapter to Eph 3:10). In Paul's time, those values included hierarchical patterns of relationships. The household was ruled by the *paterfamilias*, the male head of the family, who held all power—including the power of life and death—over every member of the house (wife, children, and slaves). That power could be, and often was, exercised oppressively. In contrast, the Church creates a new family of faith, a new set of relationships characterized by authority exercised as service and the valuing of *all* its members. As "one body in Christ," the Church upholds the dignity of all people and has a special concern for the most vulnerable members of society. Its advocacy for the rights of all people, however, can put it at odds with external cultural and political forces. This can lead to opposition to—and even hatred of—the Church.

Paul instructs the faithful about how they are to respond to the opposition and hatred of outsiders. Echoing the teaching of Jesus (cf. Matt 5:44; Luke 6:28), he exhorts the believers in Rome to "bless those who persecute you; bless and do not curse them" (12:14). Moreover, they are not to retaliate, but are to leave vengeance to God. Paul thus calls for nonviolent resistance in the face of oppressive forces (12:17–21). The Church is to advocate for justice while modeling nonviolent ways of seeking peace. Like Messiah Jesus, whose faithfulness-unto-death absorbed the violence of the cross, the *ekklēsia* is to trust in God to vindicate its commitment to justice and peace. In doing so, members of the Church may lead their opponents to a change of heart.

Paul's most famous teaching about the Church's relationship with outsiders is found in 13:1–7, where he calls for submission to governing authorities and for the payment of taxes. This passage has elicited much comment and debate. Indeed, it is not an exaggeration to say that it has exercised as much influence in the history of interpretation as any other passage in Romans. It has been enlisted to provide biblical warrant for various forms of Church-State relations—a use that would have puzzled Paul (as the applications concern historical developments he could not have imagined). It has also been appealed to by tyrants, cowing their Christian subjects to blind obedience—an appalling use that would have disgusted the Apostle. Most commentators agree that he was addressing a particular situation in Rome, one that involved controversy over taxes that had elicited much public agitation.

Having acknowledged the time-conditioned quality of the passage, it still makes several relevant points concerning the Church's relationship with the social order and with governing authorities. Paul holds the view, common in the Bible, that all governing authorities "have been instituted by God" (13:1). Underlying this view is his conviction that *God desires a just social order*. Implicit is that governing authorities should thus promote justice and order. In fact, in calling those in authority "God's servant[s]" (13:4), Paul strongly suggests that those who govern are accountable to God. This means that the Apostle ought not to be understood and interpreted as calling for "blind obedience." Those who belong to the Body of Christ must always keep in mind that their true citizenship is in heaven (Phil 3:20). Yet, because the Church exists in the world, its members should exercise their rights as citizens, engage actively in political processes, and strive always for the common good and for a more just, humane society.

Paul's benevolent description of governance in 13:3–4—it is only troublemakers who have anything to fear from rulers—is, to say the least, optimistic. To be sure, he was not naïve about how governing authorities actually operate. More than once did he suffer unjustly under their hands (e.g., Acts 16:35–40; cf. 2 Cor 11:25—being beaten with rods was an official Roman punishment). Paul's statement in 13:7 that members of the Roman house churches should give "respect to whom respect is due, honor to whom honor is due" thus says more, in my opinion, than meets the eye. While "honor" (*timē*) is owed to authorities, true *phobos* (which is better rendered as "fear," not "respect") is only owed to God (cf. the salutary "fear of the Lord"). The Apostle is quite possibly drawing on Jesus's teaching about rendering to Caesar what belongs to Caesar, and to God what belongs to God (Mark 12:13–17). The latter, of course, is the primary duty.

Paul's ultimate loyalty *is* with God, who revealed his love through Jesus. This loyalty and commitment are embedded in his fundamental proclamation: "Jesus Christ is Lord!" (Phil 2:11; cf. 2 Cor 4:5). In a time when the emperor was being acclaimed as savior and lord, this proclamation was bound to come into conflict with the imperial propaganda (cf. Acts 17:6–7). While there is no evidence of actual persecution of Christ-believers when Paul wrote the Letter to the Romans, those circumstances would change drastically in a few years. Tradition has it that he was martyred under the emperor Nero. The Apostle himself was faithful unto death.

In writing to the house churches in Rome, Paul reveals that the *ekklēsia* is the Body of Christ. By exercising its ministries in loving service, by offering hospitality and care, and by associating with the "lowly," the Church mediates Christ's presence and continues his ministry. The members of the Church are to allow love to trump differences and to encourage one another so that they can praise God with one voice. The Church by its unity-in-diversity bears witness to God's reconciling love, while also serving as an agent working for justice and peace—even (and especially) in the face of opposition.

QUESTIONS FOR PRAYER AND REFLECTION

1. How does Paul's inclusion and description of women in ministry mitigate passages like 1 Corinthians 14:34–35? In what ways can his inclusion encourage women in the Church today?

2. What analogies exist between what we know about the situation of the house churches in Rome and our situation today? How can Paul's responses be translated into today's context?

3. How might Paul's use of the olive tree metaphor help Christians to appreciate more our spiritual heritage from Judaism?

4. What is most striking to me when I consider my local worshipping community as the "body of Christ"? In what ways does my community mediate Jesus's presence and ministry?

5. Paul highlights the role of prophecy in his list of charisms in Romans. How might his understanding of this gift and its importance inspire us to appropriate it more and more?

6. How is my local community called to "associate with those who are lowly"? Who are the "lowly" (*tapeinoi*) in our midst today?

7. What are the issues that create tensions and divisions in my community of faith? How might we discern the

difference between things that people of goodwill can disagree on and those things that are nonnegotiable?

8. How am I challenged by Paul's example—following that of Jesus—of setting aside his rights in order to serve and build up other members of the Body of Christ? How can the Eucharist help in this connection?

9. What kind of collective witness does my community of faith show forth to outsiders? How engaged are we with civic and political issues? How does our belonging to Christ's Body influence that engagement?

10. How might Paul's teaching about love of enemies and nonretaliation inspire my local community to bear witness to this most difficult—yet distinctive—aspect of practicing our faith?

CONCLUSION

This brief treatment of the theological and spiritual riches in Paul's Letter to the Romans has focused explicitly on *theology* (understood in the more specific sense of seeking to know what the Apostle says about *God*), Christology, pneumatology, soteriology, and ecclesiology. All of these "ologies" are distinctions found in systematic theology.

One virtue of such an approach is to cull and give analysis to important theological topics found in Paul's most famous letter. Another virtue is that the foregoing chapters have illustrated just how intricately interconnected these topics are for him. For instance, one cannot discuss Paul's portrayal of God without explaining that God has definitively revealed his covenant love and faithfulness through his Son Jesus; has poured out his Spirit in the hearts of those who receive the gospel with faith; has acted, and continues to act, to offer salvation—understood via various aspects; and calls forth and empowers a people to bear witness to his holiness. The reader may have noticed several instances of cross-references and repetition throughout the book. While such cross-references and repetition are inevitable, they have the virtue of reinforcing major points—*repetitio mater studiorum est* ("repetition is the mother of all learning").

Admittedly, however, my approach also has some limitations. One is that the list of topics covered is far from exhaustive. A quick glance at systematic theology textbooks—and even at various presentations of Paul's theology—reveals a longer catalog of topics that are typically treated. Three topics that seem, at first glance, to be missing from my analysis are anthropology (what does Paul say about the human person and condition?), ethics (what is the best way to live?), and eschatology (what does he teach about the "last things"?). I say "at first glance" because all three topics have emerged, at times explicitly and at other times implicitly, throughout the book.

Anthropology: Reflection on who God is has ramifications for Paul's understanding of human beings, since he holds that they are created in God's image and likeness (Gen 1:26–27). Jesus, the Messiah and Son of God, not only reveals God's righteousness, love, and mercy. As the new Adam through whom God has brought about a new creation, Jesus also stands at the head of a new humanity, "the new *anthrōpos*" (Col 3:10). God's gift of the Spirit, bestowed at baptism, brings about a new reality for those who receive him: adoption as God's beloved sons and daughters, which constitutes their fundamental identity. The multifaceted ways that Paul describes God's salvation—redemption, forgiveness, justification, reconciliation, sanctification—speak to the freedom God gives to human beings to enable them to mature as living "icons," imaging his holiness to others. The Apostle's emphasis on God's impetus to form a people is a reminder of the centrality of community life for human existence. While each and every person has his or her own individual dignity and worth, human life flourishes best in the context of supporting, and being supported by, one another—such as, in the context of the Church.

Ethics: In the first chapter, I alluded to Paul's remarkable statement in 2 Corinthians 5:21 that God made Jesus, the one who did not know sin, to be a sin offering "so that in him we might become the righteousness of God." The revelation of God's righteousness is to *continue* in the lives of God's adopted sons and daughters. Messiah Jesus, the revelation of God's righteousness par excellence, shows forth what this looks like: authentic human existence, lived in obedience to God and his ways, is expressed through self-giving love for others. The Spirit empowers his recipients to take on more and more the character of Jesus—his mindset, attributes, and values—so that they may walk in the "newness of life." Having been redeemed, forgiven, and reconciled to God, they are now to embody the compassion they have received and work for reconciliation and peace among peoples. They do so more effectively when they incarnate unity-in-diversity as "one body in Christ," as local communities that mediate his presence and continue his ministry of mercy.

Eschatology: God, the Creator and Sustainer of all life who has inaugurated the new creation in Christ, will bring about the fullness of redemption, including for all the created order. God will judge everyone on the basis of his or her works, pronouncing final justification for those already justified and enabled by the Spirit to "fulfill the just requirement of the law." Jesus is the first fruits of the resurrection, and God has given the Spirit as *arrabōn* ("down payment") of the fullness of resurrection life to those who respond with faith to the gospel. Jesus reigns as Lord until the last enemy—(personified) death—has been definitively defeated, when God will be "all in all" (1 Cor 15:28). The Church gathers as the family of faith to praise and glorify God for his wondrous mercy and to anticipate their participation in the fullness of life in the presence of God.

I tell my students that it is important to keep in mind that Paul was not a systematic theologian. Not because he didn't have the capacity, but because he didn't have the time and leisure. Paul was called by the risen Lord to be an apostle, one sent to proclaim the good news to the Gentiles (Gal 1:16). From the time he encountered Jesus on the Damascus road, he tirelessly traversed thousands of miles, by land and by sea, to bring the gospel to places where it had not yet been heard. After founding communities of believers, he needed to stay in contact with them to nurture their faith. Paul came to appreciate the need to remain in communication—via personal visits, sending emissaries, and writing letters—in order to assist the new Christ-believers to mature in their faith. In short, he became a missionary and pastor.

As pastor, one of Paul's great gifts was to cut to the theological core of pastoral issues. He thus stands as the first great *practical* theologian of the Church. A classic example concerns an issue we raised briefly in the last chapter. In I Corinthians 11:17–34, Paul chastises the community in Corinth for unseemly behavior at the Lord's supper. Some wealthy members were not waiting for the poorer members to arrive; rather, they were indulgently eating and drinking from the bounty of their food and drink (at the larger feast within which the Eucharist was celebrated), leaving little or nothing for the rest. It is in this context that the Apostle cites Jesus's words over the bread and wine, the earliest scriptural witness of these words. His purpose in doing so is to remind the Corinthians of what it is they are commemorating in the Eucharist: Jesus's giving over, in love, his life for them. The selfish behavior of some in the community is therefore completely incommensurate with what they are claiming to celebrate.

Paul's penchant for theological practicality perdures to this day. For instance, recall from the treatment in chapter 3 that his virtue lists (e.g., I Cor 13:4–7; Col 3:12–17) provide word portraits of Jesus's character and attributes. Individuals and communities can gauge their progress in the life of the Spirit by examining themselves against these lists. The one set forth in Gal 5:22–23—"love, joy, peace, patience, kindness, generosity, faithfulness, gentleness, and self-control"—makes crystal clear the "fruit" the Spirit seeks to bear in his recipients. Similarly, Paul's list of ministries and the manner in which they are to be carried out (Rom 12:6–8) provides a helpful template against which communities of faith can measure themselves. Are we attentive to God's presence? Do we discern God's Word for our particular circumstances? Are we encouraging and generous? Are we merciful in reaching out to those in need—both members and nonmembers?

Another example of the practicality of Paul's teaching is how the indicative (that is, the "fact") of salvation elicits certain imperatives. We who have been shown mercy and have been forgiven are in turn to become more compassionate and forbearing (e.g., Eph 4:32). We who have been reconciled to God are to become ambassadors of reconciliation (e.g., 2 Cor 5:18–20). We who have been redeemed are to exercise our freedom in loving service and seek to relieve others of their burdens (e.g., Gal 6:2). We who, in God's love, have been justified by Jesus's cross—even when we were God's enemies—are to be agents of God's nonviolent love in the world, even toward our enemies and persecutors (Rom 12:14, 17–21).

Finally, and here we come full circle, we return to Paul's practical way of reading Scripture. He holds that Jesus is the *telos*, the goal and fulfillment, of the Jewish Scriptures and of the promises of God contained therein. But Paul is also convinced that the story of Jesus, and thus the story contained in Scripture, *continues* in the life of the Church. In the introduction, we saw how the Apostle reads Psalm 69—the story of the righteous sufferer whose faithfulness to God's ways is completely vindicated—as referring not only to Jesus but also to the situation of the believers in the Roman house churches. The sacred words were "written for our instruction." So, too, were the words of Isaiah 49:8 that Paul quotes in 2 Corinthians 6:2:

> At an acceptable time I [the LORD] have listened to
> you,
> and on a day of salvation I have helped you.

As is his wont, he goes on to contemporize these words: "See, *now* is the acceptable time; see, *now* is the day of salvation!" And this "now" continues to this very day. Indeed, we can be most grateful to St. Paul for the life-giving theological and spiritual riches *written for our instruction.*

NOTES

INTRODUCTION

1. Along with Romans, these four letters, as well as I Thessalonians and Philemon, are regarded by nearly all New Testament scholars as deriving from Paul and his ministry.

2. Second Thessalonians also fits into this category of a "disputed" letter, regarded by many as "deutero-Pauline." The so-called "Pastoral Epistles" (1–2 Tim and Titus) are considered by the vast majority of scholars to be from a later hand.

1. GOD

1. Unless otherwise indicated, biblical references are to Paul's Letter to the Romans.

2. Jerome used the Hebrew text as the basis of his translation of the Old Testament into Latin.

3. "Christ" is from the Greek word *Christos*, meaning the "anointed one"—that is, the Messiah.

4. Paul did not envision a situation where the Church and Israel would become two distinct entities for nearly two millennia. It is important for Christians to appreciate that, according to him, the Church does not replace Israel. He is no supersessionist. (See chapter 5.)

2. JESUS

1. This version is called the Septuagint. It is signified by the Roman numeral LXX because of the tradition that it was produced by seventy Jewish translators.

2. The quoted words are from the NRSV. However, I have added the diacritical marker (/) to indicate better the text's structural balance.

3. Jews view their Scriptures as having three divisions: the Law (Torah), the prophets (Nevi'im), and the writings (Ketuvim). Their name for the Scriptures, *Tanakh*, is an acronym from these three divisions. Cf. Luke 24:44, where the risen Jesus refers to these three parts of Scripture as "the law of Moses, the prophets, and the psalms."

4. Psalm 69 is also alluded to in the passion narratives in the Synoptic Gospels. See Mark 15:23 (and the parallel texts in Matthew and Luke), an allusion to Psalm 69:21. Cf. also John 2:17, a citation of Psalm 69:9a, the line that immediately precedes the one Paul quotes.

5. Paul focuses on the figure of Adam, not Eve, because it allows for a more direct comparison with Jesus.

3. SPIRIT

1. Insofar as it is necessary to use a pronoun in connection with "Spirit," I have chosen the masculine form to convey the sense that, for Paul, the Spirit is a *personal* divine presence and power—even though, grammatically, the Greek *to pneuma* is neuter. But it is also important to point out that the Spirit is not gendered.

2. Elsewhere, Paul uses "God's temple" to describe the (local) community of believers (1 Cor 3:16; 2 Cor 6:16). This reflects his typical emphasis on communities rather than on individuals.

3. *Saul* was his given Semitic name; *Paulos* was his Greek name (in Latin, *Paulus*).

4. Galatians 2:20 is another instance of the phrase *pistis Christou*. See the first section in chapter 2 for translating it as Christ's faithfulness.

5. In addition to Paul's two uses, the verb *metamorphoō* appears only two other times in the New Testament, both in connection with Jesus's transfiguration (cf. Matt 17:2; Mark 9:2).

4. SALVATION

1. I capitalize the Greek terms in order to convey Paul's personification of sin and death.

2. Paul's prophet-like critique of Israel can be a source of self-examination for us whose identity and vocation is to be the sacrament (that is, the embodiment) of Christ's love in the world (see *Lumen Gentium* 48).

3. The footnote in NRSV has "as a sin offering" as an alternative translation to "to deal with sin."

4. Paul can speak of God as judge (14:10), of Christ as judge (1 Cor 4:4), and of God judging through Christ (2:16).

5. Cf. NRSV's alternative translation of Galatians 2:16.

6. Moreover, as Pope Francis so prophetically reminds us, the task of reconciliation also means reconciliation with the environment, working for ecological restoration.

5. CHURCH

1. Scholars conjecture that the cause of the exile was disputes among Jews, believers in Christ and nonbelievers, over claims being made about Jesus as Messiah and Lord.

2. Largely on the basis of texts like 1 Corinthians 14:34–35. Undoubtedly, Paul was a man of his times, and those times were marked by patriarchy. This makes his inclusion of women all the more remarkable—as was the case with Jesus in his ministry (cf. Luke 8:1–3).

3. The labels "strong" and "weak" represent the former's perspective. Paul aligns himself with the "strong" in 15:1, though the NRSV's rendering of that passage is misleading; it reads, literally, "We who are strong ought to bear with the weaknesses [not failings] of those who are not strong." The Greek text does not have "failings."

4. One possible scenario involved meat sold in the marketplace. Such meat often came from temple sacrifices.

5. The Eucharist was celebrated within the context of a larger *agape* meal. The issue in Corinth involved wealthier members in the community eating and drinking before others (e.g., slaves) were able to arrive, creating division and shaming poorer members.